TRACING
the
HISTORY
of
YOUR
*H*OUSE

*B*RENDA GREYSMITH

Hodder & Stoughton
A MEMBER OF THE HODDER HEADLINE GROUP

Acknowledgements

The Publishers would like to thank Taurus Graphics for the drawings and the following for permission to reproduce the photographs in this volume:

John Barlow, front cover.

Edifice, back cover & spine; p. 1; p. 2 (both); p. 8; p. 15 (bottom); p. 20 (bottom); p. 22 (both); p. 25; p. 26 (top); p. 32 (top); p. 36; p.44 (bottom); p. 45; p. 48; p. 50; p. 51; p. 53; p. 58; p.64 (top); p. 71 (both); p. 72; p. 73 (both); p. 77; p. 78; p. 79; p. 81; p. 82; p. 83; p. 84 (both); p. 86; p. 87 (all); p. 88.

Dick & Jean Randall p. 4; p. 7; p. 40; p. 57.

Dave West Photography p. 14 (both); p. 15 (top); p. 44 (bottom); p. 56; p. 61; p. 62.

Paul Freestone Photography p. 16; p. 23.

Elizabeth Whiting & Associates p. 19; p. 91 (top).

Ed Buziak/House & Interiors Photographic Features Agency p. 20 (top); p. 93 (top); p. 100 (bottom).

Tony Herbert p. 21; p. 47; p. 93 (bottom).

Savills Chartered Surveyors p. 26 (bottom); p. 96.

Andrew M. Jenkinson p. 43; p. 64 (bottom); p. 65; p.66.

Elizabeth Carcasson p. 46; p.49; p. 63; p. 67.

David Markson/House & Interiors Photographic Features Agency p. 52; p. 100 (top).

John Fidler p. 69.

G. Jackson & Son p. 94; p. 97.

National Trust Photographic Library p. 95.

English Heritage Photographic Library p. 99.

Cataloguing in Publication Data is available from the British Library

ISBN 0 340 591692 Paperback
     0 340 620722 Hardback

First published 1994
Impression number 10 9 8 7 6 5 4 3 2 1
Year   1998 1997 1996 1995 1994

Copyright © 1994 Brenda Greysmith

Typeset by Litho Link Ltd., Welshpool, Powys, Wales.
Printed in Great Britain for Hodder & Stoughton Educational, a division of Hodder Headline Plc, 338 Euston Road, London NW1 3BH by Thomson Litho Limited.

CONTENTS

$\mathcal{I}$NTRODUCTION

How old is your house? This may seem a straightforward question and one that will have a simple answer, but a house is complex structure in a landscape with a long history, and once you start looking into its past you will find that just knowing the date the foundations were laid is only a small part of a fascinating story.

So this book is concerned with tracing the history of your house rather than just pointing you towards the date when it was built. There are good reasons for this approach. A house is changed and adapted throughout its lifetime and the 'modernisations' of previous owners will give you insights into how their aspirations have altered your home's present appearance. Also, a house is affected by its surroundings so, even if it is quite new, the previous ownership of the land and what was there before may have dictated its current state.

The building itself will tell you much of its history if you can understand its language. Its architectural style, the design of features and changes in the use of building materials surround you and are on hand to be studied every day whenever you have time to turn your attention to them. In addition, there is documentary evidence readily available to you which should furnish information on the house itself and perhaps on its former owners. Genealogy, tracing the history of your family, has become an enormously popular pastime, and many of its techniques can be adapted to find out who lived in your house before you – perhaps even something of their lives and characters.

Do not assume that you are going to have to start from scratch and that no research will ever have been done on your house or its occupants before. If findings do already exist, it will not reduce the fun of the search – research is always open ended, and there will be more to find out and fascinating details to fill in. So enjoy any leads that others have found for you.

The most obvious sources of information can often be the most useful and entertaining. Chatting to the neighbours can fill you in on the area's history (though allow for some poetic licence), and the estate agent who sold you the house may know a considerable amount about its history. Estate agents have become a bit like mothers-in-law in that they suffer from a bad press and weak jokes, but they often have a good knowledge of the houses in their area. The solicitor who handled the conveyancing may also have turned up interesting information during the searches. Amateur historians (or professional ones) may have researched the locality, your house or even its previous owners; your public library is likely to have a wealth of documentation on the area, its past and personalities, and to be able to point you to further sources of information.

For all your areas of research you will need to play the detective and work patiently, with no preconceptions as to what you may find and a lively mind prepared to take off in new directions when unexpected doors are opened.

1

ARCHITECTURAL EVIDENCE
– GENERAL TIPS

CLUES AND RED HERRINGS

Dating your house from how it looks is a fascinating but often imprecise science. There are several reasons for the elusive nature of the task. First, while a new fashion nowadays spreads like wildfire, in the past it might take generations, even centuries, for a change in architectural taste to filter across the country and down the social scale. So a certain style might indicate an early date in a house built for London gentry, but quite a late one in a Cumbrian farmhouse. In addition, each age has had its own nostalgia for styles that were old-fashioned or reproduction. The Victorians and Edwardians had a particular passion for recycling the architecture of the past in this way.

But the most challenging part of such a project is that very few houses were ever built and then just left alone, with no further tinkering to their structure or appearance. Buildings need repair, of course, and they are also updated with improved facilities and materials. Sometimes reconstruction went considerably further and new houses were built on top of old cellars, or were rebuilt following a fire which had left perhaps only the stonework chimneys standing.

Lifestyles have always changed too, and in response to this, houses have been adapted to meet the new needs of the occupants. Later extensions may hide an early form of wall construction, or new interior divisions obscure the original house plan. Sometimes these changes actually set out to deceive: when a style fell out of fashion, a

A battlemented porch and Gothic tracery for the door, but this Gloucestershire house is actually nineteenth-century revival style.

Datestones may not necessarily show the year of building. Here a doorcase in Askham, Cumbria, incorporates the date 1674 and an escutcheon with the initials HLD.

A less naïve datestone sits below a sundial on a house in Edinburgh. The figure of 1892 is surrounded by texts in Greek and the local vernacular.

house might be refaced to look as though it had been built in the latest vogue.

Occasionally, a building has what seems to be incontrovertible proof of its date of building in the form of an engraved *datestone* embedded in the exterior of a wall. But even this evidence should be treated with caution. A datestone sometimes commemorated another event, such as a marriage within the family, rather than the building of the house. Alternatively, it may mark the time when the property was renovated or extended, or even be a fake or have come from elsewhere.

The scientific wood dating technique, *dendrochronology*, can be used to find the age of timbers, and several univerities and private firms will date a wood sample for a set fee. But here again there can be no absolute certainty that the timber has not been reused from another, earlier house.

So how do you spot a red herring? Awareness of the general building styles and practices through the centuries, the most usual forms of updating carried out by occupants, and unlikely finishes or materials can give you clues as to whether something was original to the house or not. For example, anything that seems unusual for your part of the country should be regarded with suspicion if you believe your home to be pre-nineteenth century – the use of building materials from close to home was the norm before cheap transport became available in the 1800s.

Materials may be specifically designed to look older than they really are, with an 'antiqued' finish – often rather overdone. Bricks are a favourite subject for this treatment. Beams are also often faked with planks, or plastic or glassfibre replicas, or simply painted on to a facade to simulate timber frame. Check that a beam is serving a structural purpose, and not merely a decorative later addition.

Material may have been taken from elsewhere and reused, for the idea of architectural salvage is not a new one. From the late eighteenth century onwards, there was considerable interest in the building styles of the past and materials were reused in new buildings with a vaguely imitative style, or to add a 'repro' extension to an existing house. Although unconcerned with such questions of fashion and style, poorer houses constructed close to abandoned structures, such as monasteries, would also have made good use of this handy local source of supply.

Salvaged material may give itself away by its incongruous level of quality, or detailing or structural marks which do not seem logical for their current site. Unless they are just ornamental, salvaged or reproduction, materials used recently will have had to comply to modern building regulations. Thus windows will be larger and ceilings higher than those of an old cottage; chimneys will be smaller and the roof will incorporate insulation.

$\mathcal{T}$YPICAL CHANGES

Spotting changes that have been made to a house since it was first constructed may be made easier by examining the back of the building. This is less likely to have been altered to keep up with fashion, and any extensions will probably have been added on without attempting to deceive. The back may reveal the house's original materials, structure, window and door styles, or display the rambling character of an early building which has been hidden behind a later symmetrical street frontage.

A house's *roof structure* tends to go unaltered, so the roof space is the next area to check out. But here, too, you may find evidence of alterations: very early roofs, with carved timbers which were meant to be seen, and smoke-blackened timbers from the days before chimneys, may have been modernised by the installation of a ceiling below them. Perhaps the whole roof has been raised, dormer windows may have been inserted, or the roof pitch flattened to facilitate the use of the attic – a popular practice in the eighteenth and nineteenth centuries. At least recent changes should be easily distinguishable, for new roof timbers, installed since the nineteenth century's mechanisation of the timber industry, will look machine-cut and regular.

In old roofs, the covering material was attached directly to the roof structure's battens or boards and, until the nineteenth century, the overlap of slates and tiles was relied on to provide a waterproof layer. In early houses, a layer of mortar reinforced with hair or vegetation ('torching') was sometimes used as an imperfect second line of weatherproofing which would keep the rain out – at least for a while.

Roof coverings have a shorter life than most building materials and are very likely to have been renewed. Like timber, early roof covering materials will have a hand-made appearance. While hand-made tiles are still produced in small quantities, roofing materials are now generally machine-made and will have a uniform look. Tiling details have changed, too, with a general trend towards purpose-made special tiles for jobs that would have taken the roofer's time and skill in the past. At roof edges or verges, for example, half slates or tiles were used until the nineteenth century; in modern times, slate-and-half or tile-and-half sizes are used to give better weather resistance.

Walling materials, too, may not be what they seem. For example, the surface may merely be a facing, perhaps added long after the house was built. This is particularly true of timber framing: during the seventeenth and eighteenth centuries older buildings were often covered up to make them both more fashionable and weatherproof.

Timber-frame houses may lie concealed behind a façade of other materials.

Chimneys tend to deteriorate far more quickly than the main walling, because of their exposure to the weather and combustion gases, and are likely to have been reconstructed.

Materials may have been salvaged from another, earlier building. In brick and stone buildings, checking the consistency of the mortar should at least tell you whether the construction work has been done before the end of the nineteenth century, for up to this date the mortar would have incorporated lime and will be softer and more crumbly than more modern mixes.

Windows and doors have always been among the most frequently changed parts of a house, and they continue to be so as fashions dictate new shapes and materials. So, their style is not necessarily a reliable indication of the age of your house, and you should be aware of clues that may show that they are not the original ones.

Consider whether their current positioning seems to fit the plan and style of the house and look out for evidence of any changes. Cracks in plaster and bulges or recesses in walls can indicate that openings have been blocked up, while the later addition of an opening is also likely to have disturbed the surrounding wall. Sometimes careful excavation may even reveal a window, complete with glazing, under the plaster.

In all types of houses, the surround is less likely to have been altered than the door or window itself. The original position of a door in a timber-framed house, for example, will be shown by an absence of the peg holes and mortices in the uprights which formed the door opening. Around a window, evidence of shutters may remain. Sometimes the original windows are still in place but have been adapted: many houses have sash windows where the glazing bars have been removed to accommodate larger panes of glass (possibly in Victorian times when big sheets of mass-produced glass became available).

On the other hand, genuinely old doors and windows may not have always been sited in your house, but have been taken from another building. Alternatively, modern reproduction ones may have been introduced. These are generally distinguishable by their rather mechanical appearance, and sometimes their comparatively lightweight construction and poor sense of traditional proportions. Old doors, for example, are often wider and shorter than their modern equivalents, while today's glazing bars tend to be thicker and clumsier than those of the past. Occasionally, a more convincing copy has been specially made with old materials.

Many less structural components of the *interior* may be later additions or decoration, or may have been brought to the house second-hand. Even a staircase may have been moved and modified when a house was extended. Evidence of these types of changes to the interior should be weighed up in conjunction with the plan form of the house and the structure of the roof.

If the plan of your house seems 'quirky', it may be a *conversion*, a practice that has not been limited to the recent past. Schools, workshops, barns, churches and chapels have all been converted to domestic accommodation over the centuries. The ground floor of many seventeenth-century town and village houses, originally built for residential use, were later converted into shops. Yet during the twentieth century, as small communities have come to rely on larger towns for their shopping, village stores have tended to become purely residential.

Large houses are often subdivided as their wealthy owners die out or move on. After the Parliamentary Enclosures Act of the eighteenth century, for example, new farmhouses were built in the enclosed fields, while the old ones situated in village streets were divided up for farmworkers.

$\int$ITING

The oldest *townhouses* are usually in the centre of the settlement, for most towns and villages started with just a few houses and spread outwards. So it is generally true to say that outer suburbs will have developed later. However, sometimes settlements have grown out so much that they have absorbed other villages and as a result have nuclei of older houses outside the main centre. Street names can sometimes provide an indication of whether the area was an independent centre with its own markets.

Medieval townhouse plots were usually narrow, running back from the street frontage sometimes to a parallel lane beyond. Later townhouses, and village houses where space was not at such a premium, were built on wider plots, running lengthwise alongside the road or village green.

The siting of *farmhouses* varies from the isolated hill farm, through locations in small hamlets, to their presence on village streets. Village farmhouses probably date from the days of open field systems before the land enclosures of the eighteenth century. Those within hamlets usually occur in areas of pastoral farming, such as the mountainous regions of Wales, although this pattern may also be the result of the settlement dwindling down in size from a larger village.

Isolated farmhouses were often built on waste land and can date from many different periods. The surrounding field shapes will give some clues: the farm may be early if they are small and irregular, large and regular fields may indicate a date before the eighteenth century, when such land was enclosed. (Although field patterns are changing now with the removal of hedges, the old pattern can be traced on early 1:2500 Ordnance Survey maps). In addition to influencing the siting of farmhouses proper, the Enclosures Act also precipitated the building of a rash of small, poor cottages on the verges of turnpike roads and the edges of the still unenclosed heaths and commonland, by the many displaced farmers and farm labourers who had lost their holdings.

HOUSES FOR CRAFTS AND INDUSTRIES

Until the last century, every area had its own craftsmen, as we would say now 'working from home', in custom-built accommodation. Sometimes the original function of the building is commemorated in its name. *Wheelwright's workshops* and *blacksmith's forges* were numerous, catering for the enormous numbers of horses and the carriages which they pulled. Usually these craftsmen's workshops adjoined their houses, which made them simple to convert to a single unit after railways and cars revolutionised transport and the need for such businesses dwindled.

The miller had a vital role in the community, too, and *wind* and *water mills* have a long history, although most surviving mills date from the eighteenth and nineteenth centuries. There was usually a house attached to each mill, and this often remains even if the mill itself has gone.

Spinning and weaving were important activities in some areas, with work being carried out at home even after the Industrial Revolution. Good light was important for this fine work, and the houses of textile workers often have long, horizontal windows to provide maximum daylight to large rooms on the upper floor.

The development of transport is well documented and brought about the building of specialised housing which can be relatively easily dated. Turnpike roads were built during the late eighteenth and early nineteenth centuries, at the same time as their *toll houses*.

Prior's Mill, Astley, Hereford and Worcester. Water mills, like windmills, smithies and wheelwrights' workshops were common working buildings before the industrial and transport revolutions, but many of those which have survived have been converted for domestic use.

7

Situated close to the road, these often have an unusual shape (perhaps octagonal or hexagonal) and might have large bay windows to give a good view of the road.

Toll houses were often many sided to give a good view of the road. This example is at Tavistock.

The same period saw the creation of an extensive network of canals across the country. Along their banks, *canal cottages* for lock keepers, bridge keepers, toll clerks, labourers and craftsmen appeared, often in the special style of the particular canal company. In a less romantic setting, extensive *railway housing* for workers was built close to stations during the middle of the nineteenth century.

Society has always needed a refuge for the needy, so *almshouses* have a long history: early examples, built on a communal plan, date from the Middle Ages. After the dissolution of the monasteries in the sixteenth century, almshouses were often built by the local gentry and wealthy merchants. Increasingly, they were built as a series of individual units, often with a warden's house and sometimes a chapel. The appearance of almshouses can be misleading, for they were often built in a style that was old-fashioned, but many have datestones and, as 'public buildings' they are also likely to be well documented.

All the medieval towns had their *alehouses*, which probably (like the houses of the times) took the form of an open hall for communal eating and drinking. Until the sixteenth century Reformation, the church also brewed and sold ale and the church house might provide a large, first-floor room, approached by an external staircase, with stores and service rooms below on the ground floor. Since then, taverns have evolved continuously, so they follow no standard pattern, although numerous new ones were built during the eighteenth and nineteenth centuries. Until the nineteenth century, brewing was carried out locally and alehouses would have their own buildings for this process.

Inns catering for travellers had been run by religious orders in medieval times, but after the Reformation they passed into secular hands. Again, they were similar in layout to the houses of the time, with the larger inns following a courtyard plan, with access via a high, arched entrance. During the sixteenth century, they followed the trend in domestic building away from open dormitories towards smaller rooms, perhaps with the extra privacy gained by providing access to bedrooms via gallery corridors.

From the sixteenth to the nineteenth century, inns continued to grow in importance as stage-coach travel developed and trade expanded. The courtyard plan remained common; larger inns might have two, the first surrounded by the public rooms and the second by the service rooms and stables. With the coming of the railways in the nineteenth century, inns started to lose their traditional role; however, some became hotels catering for a society that now had more leisure time and had begun to travel for pleasure.

MAKING A RECORD

Making a record will encourage you to look with attention at details which you might otherwise miss and help you to build up a coherent picture of your house. When you have finished the drawing of your house you may even be able to work out the original form of the building and how it has been altered.

Sometimes it is possible to make a series of sketches showing the building at different stages in its development, although it is easy to be misled by wishful thinking.

Begin by making a quick tour round to get your bearings and a general feeling of shapes and boundaries, plus some idea of what you might want to record in detail. It can be useful to carry out this first stage with a partner: one person on their own is more likely to miss something. Then, when you are feeling unhurried and have plenty of time to give the project, go slowly round the house making notes and photographing any interesting details, working systematically from left to right and clockwise.

Photographs do not have to look professional so you will not have to splash out on lots of expensive equipment, although certain items will make things easier. A flashgun will cope with most interior shots, used in conjunction with a fast colour film. A zoom lens will allow you to take details and wide-angled shots in a cramped situation; a telephoto lens will enable you to take shots of chimneys and ridge tiles without endangering life and limb. Photos should be as near to true elevations as possible and, if you have an automatic camera, take care to point it directly at and fairly close to anything which has light behind it or the camera will adjust to the brightness and put the detail you want to show into shadow.

Take notes about anything that will not be shown in your photographs; you can back them up with drawings of any features. Label your pages to ensure that you know what room or feature is being dealt with.

Pace out the rooms and sketch out rough plans of each floor of the house, remembering to show wall thicknesses. It is easiest to use squared paper and work in pencil so that you can keep rubbing out until you are satisfied that the proportions are roughly correct. Go over the pencil lines in ink and sketch in details, such as windows and doors, fireplaces and changes in materials. Next, sketch cross-sections and an external elevation in the same way. These rough drawings can now be the basis for writing in actual measurements; the use of a contrasting pen colour for dimensions will help avoid the plan becoming confusing.

It is important to approach the measuring unhurriedly and systematically. Work from the left to right or clockwise in each room and measure from the left-hand wall. Initially, you can ignore doors and windows and concentrate on the walls, adding the smaller measurements once the running lengths are established. Diagonal measurements of rooms should be taken as well as wall lengths, so that they can be cross checked. For sections and elevations, it is necessary to measure ceiling heights, window cill and head heights, door head heights, and floor thicknesses (which can be measured at staircase wells). Changes in floor level should also be noted.

If the roof space is accessible, it is relatively easy to obtain the angle of the roof pitch, by measuring the height of the ridge, and to measure the sizes and positions of roof timbers (especially important if the construction could be early). If the roof space is inaccessible, the height of the ridge can be estimated from the gable end.

In a brick building, the height can be obtained by counting the rows of bricks. Modern brickwork has four courses to 1 foot, but in older buildings, brick courses may vary so it is necessary to take a sample and use this to make the calculation. Other materials, such as drainpipes, tiles and stone blocks, may also come in regularly repeating sizes and assist in estimating external measurements. You should always check the basic module's measurement whenever possible, but this type of estimation can be surprisingly accurate and very useful.

With the survey complete, the next task is drawing it up. This is best done on tracing paper, so that when the ground floor has been done it can be used as a basis for the upper floors – though you must remember to check measurements against it. The method of drawing is this: draw a line representing the room's width to the required scale, then from one end of the line use compasses to describe an arc the length of the side wall and from the other end of the line describe another arc the length of room's diagonal measurement. This method can be used to fix the other corner of the room which can be checked against the survey measurements.

First produce a pencil draft, concentrating on accuracy, to show all your plans, sections and elevations to the chosen scale. Then cut out the separate drawings and re-arrange them into a compact composition that leaves space for the titles, notes, scale and north point. Secure them in position with sticky tape and trace neatly over this patchwork version. Pen mark errors on tracing paper can be removed by scraping gently and carefully with a sharp razor blade, on tracing film they can be removed with a little water. Plans of old buildings, especially timber-framed ones, can look unconvincingly regular if the lines are ruled; a well-controlled freehand line may look more sympathetic.

Despite their large size, copies of plans are easily produced by either Xerox or Dyeline and both services are available to the public. Look in your Yellow Pages under reprographic services. Such copies can be useful for a variety of purposes, not least of which is the addition of any features discovered at a later date, during work on the house. A copy should also be kept with the deeds for the interest and guidance of the house's future owners. In addition, if the house is of historic interest, the local authority and record office, or the local museum and historical society would probably be grateful for copies of your drawings.

EQUIPMENT

For the survey you will need:

- camera;
- notebook;
- sketch pad, or plain or squared paper, and a firm clip board;
- pencils and a good quality eraser;
- 100-foot (or metric equivalent) linen or steel tape;
- 5-foot expanding wooden rod or a 6- to 10-foot retractable tape that stays rigid when opened;
- torch;
- binoculars.

Although it is possible to carry out a survey on your own, it is much easier if there are other people to hold the other end of tape measures and note down measurements.

For drawing up your findings you will need:

- drawing board;
- T-square;
- set square;
- scale rule;
- compass;
- pentel pen, or Rapidograph and Indian ink;
- tracing paper or polyester tracing film.

For drawing up it is best to work on a drawing board with a T-square and a set square. Small portable drawing boards are available. Adjustable angle set squares are useful as old buildings rarely have right angle corners. Compasses and spring bows – the last for small arcs, such as door swings and a 6-inch scale, graded in imperial and metric, will be needed.

The scale of the final drawing is normally 1:100 (or 8 feet to 1 inch) for larger buildings and 1:50 (or 4 feet to 1 inch) for smaller ones.

2

$\mathcal{O}$UTLINE OF HISTORIC ARCHITECTURAL STYLES

$\mathcal{T}$HE VERNACULAR

Vernacular architecture is the term used to describe buildings, both domestic and agricultural, built of local materials, uninfluenced (largely) by fashion and relying on traditional solutions to practical problems. Houses of this type tend to be more difficult to date than those which follow a fashionable style; vernacular houses were constructed over many centuries, from earliest times right up until the late 1800s, with few variations to provide helpful clues. The smaller the house, the poorer its occupant and the less likely it was to be well built. So surviving medieval examples are those that were once the property of knights; those still standing from the seventeenth century include houses owned by yoemen; while those from the nineteenth century belonged to a wide social range.

The *Great Rebuilding*, which took place in most areas of England and Wales at various times between the fifteenth and eighteenth centuries, saw the demolition or alteration of many vernacular houses. It also marked the beginnings of 'polite' architecture, influenced by fashionable classical style and professional architects. Even so, while polite details, such as sash windows, began to appear in vernacular buildings, the latter did continue until mass production and improved transport systems made standard building materials and styles ubiquitous nationwide.

Vernacular architecture encompasses buildings of timber frame, whether exposed, rendered or clad, plus buildings of stone from local quarries, flint, brick from the local brickworks and the various forms of clay. Of these materials, timber frame and brickwork are probably the easiest to give at least a rough date. The marvellous

Vernacular houses were common from earliest times through to the late 1800s. This black-and-white, timber-framed house is in Eardisland in the West Midlands. It has an impressive stepped chimney.

A dovecote in the gable-end – a practical approach for this Herefordshire cottage built in the local stone.

A Devonshire long house near Dartmoor, originally built with a byre to house animals to one side of the human occupants' living accommodation.

A stone-built, thatched cottage in an Oxfordshire village. The better finished stone has been used for the front of the building.

15

An Oxfordshire house built in 1649 on the site of a chapel and leper hospital which had been razed to the ground in the Civil War. This long rectangular building was originally four separate dwellings for eight almsmen.

variety of the country's stone houses often says more about the geology of different areas than about their period of construction: mellow Cotswold stone and rough Highland rubble are the hallmarks of their districts.

Each area's vernacular buildings have their own characteristics and their own timescales, and cannot be given general dates. It is well worth seeking out information from your public library, local history group and vernacular architecture group whose knowledge of the immediate locality could provide more specific information.

Just as the building of vernacular houses finally faded out at the end of the nineteenth century, its style saw a self-conscious rebirth in the *Vernacular Revival* championed by architects in the wake of the Arts and Crafts Movement. Sprawling middle-class houses were designed by such nationally famous architects as Philip Webb, William Lethaby, Charles Voysey, Sir George Gilbert Scott and Sir Edwin Lutyens; the buildings might incorporate timber frame, local stone and small-paned windows. Their work had a strong influence on the 1930's 'Tudorbethan' suburban semi-detached houses and terraces, with their timber frame patterns, leaded lights and herringbone brickwork.

*P*OLITE ARCHITECTURE

The division between vernacular and the more style-conscious polite architecture did not really exist before the fifteenth century. The more modest cottages were built simply and with poor quality materials while the manorial hall houses of the rich were larger, more complex and substantial. Ecclesiastical styles affected domestic building, with the unpretentious carving and pointed arches of the *Gothic* style appearing in some houses of the period. But, from that time, the trend away from communal living space towards the privacy of separate living quarters started to change the design of houses. This not only coincided with a desire among the increasing numbers of the wealthy to show off their status, but also the emergence of *Renaissance* influence.

Medieval design mixed with the new approach in a transitionary period that could be said to last through to the early eighteenth century. In its early days, the *Tudor* Renaissance saw an increased use of romantic picturesque detail and more flamboyant carving. Patterned brickwork, huge and elaborately-shaped chimneys attested a new interest in the visual arts, a new burst of creativity and a turning from the ecclesiastical to the secular. During the reigns of Elizabeth I and James I, these tendencies were intensified, with designs becoming more individual, vibrant and dynamic. Knowledge of classical designs existed, but they were used as just one ingredient in an exotic mixture.

During the sixteenth and seventeenth centuries, the influence of the Renaissance created a stronger and stronger desire for symmetry and formality. Many houses were altered and enlarged, and many new ones were built reflecting the change in style. By the end of the seventeenth century, *Queen Anne* architecture still retained some of the exuberance of Elizabethan times, but was tempering it with the restraint that was to be a feature of the Georgians. As the eighteenth century began, the influence of Dutch fashion and a liking for red brick reflected the reign of Mary and William of Orange. Chimneys still towered over the roofline, but windows had lost their horizontal emphasis and were becoming taller and more regularly placed.

When George I took the throne, the Renaissance influence was widespread, with non-vernacular houses having a compact rectangular plan, a symmetrical façade and classical detailing. The population, from squire, through farmer and tradesman, to country parson, aspired to live in a *Georgian* style house based on the temple architecture of an ancient Mediterranean civilisation.

The triumphal arch and classical columns were adopted with enthusiasm and adapted to homely middle-class taste. Pedimented porches, fanlights, sash windows and pilasters blended with a new

Style	Period (simplified)	Period (divided)	Monarch	Date
Gothic	Tudor	Elizabethan	Elizabeth	1600
	Jacobean	Jacobean	James I	
Baroque		Carolean	Charles I	1650
		Cromwellian	Commonwealth	
		Restoration Carolean or Late Stuart	Charles II	
			James II	
	William & Mary	Wm & Mary	Wm & Mary	1700
		William III	William III	
Rococo	Queen Anne	Queen Anne	Anne	
		Early Georgian	George I	
	Early Georgian		George II	1750
		Mid Georgian		
Neo Classical	Late Georgian	Late Georgian	George III	1800
Regency	Regency	Regency	George IV	
		William IV	William IV	
Eclectic (including Neogothic)	Victorian	Early Victorian		1850
		Mid-Victorian	Victoria	
Arts & Crafts		Late Victorian		1900
Art Nouveau	Edwardian	Edwardian	Edward VII	
Art Deco + Vernacular Rev.	Modern	Inter-War	George V ← Edward VIII	
Modern		Post-War	George VI	1950

spatial awareness, where aesthetics often overrode practical convenience. The roof was half hidden behind a parapet with a cornice of brick or stucco. Classical details, which appeared in a series of architectural pattern books published in the first half of the eighteenth century, were readily copied by provincial builders who understood little of the design principles but wanted to add fashionable ornament to their handiwork.

Classically influenced design also affected planning on a far larger scale, and this period saw terraces, crescents and squares conceived as fine architectural compositions, a building legacy which was carried on, though less strikingly, into the last century.

As the Georgian style lost some of its inventiveness and became more standardised, a desire for the *Picturesque* affected all types of houses. In the second half of the eighteenth century, there was a

A Queen Anne front was added in the eighteenth century to make this Worcestershire house one imposing whole. Originally it was two separate seventeenth-century cottages.

An eighteenth-century house in
Devizes, once part of a low, half-
timbered dwelling with a jettied
upper floor. The main building is
cruck-framed.

Double-fronted Georgian terraced
houses in Ludlow, Shropshire.

Thwaite House, Leeds, built for the local mill owner in 1823-25.

reaction against the disciplined elevations of Georgian houses and various, more frivolous styles developed. Historical influences could be seen in the recreation of the battlements and turrets of less-settled times, while mock ruins and follies added instant antiquity. But the period mingled more exotic influences too: Chinese, Indian, Egyptian and Moorish detailing also appeared.

From the middle to the end of the eighteenth century, one particular style, the *Gothick*, was inspired by contemporary literature and light-heartedly picked out just the trimmings of historical

Thin glazing bars and pointed arches give an early nineteenth-century Gothick style to a house in Bristol.

design, adapting them with more than a touch of fantasy. It took the pointed arches of pre-Renaissance times, for example, but shunned any return to the medieval house plan. In contrast to the heavy-handed approach of the Victorian historicism that was to follow, Georgian Gothick was sheer high spirits.

Out of this environment grew the delicate *Regency* style, which combined the unorthodox with an unsurpassed lightness of touch. Thin glazing bars, intricate ironwork for balconies and porches, curved bays, light-painted stucco, and low-pitched roofs were among its hallmarks, still to be seen in many of the country's coastal resorts.

Royal York Crescent in Clifton, Bristol, a splendid example of the ironwork balconies popular at seaside resorts in the late eighteenth century.

The predominant housing of the nineteenth century was the *Victorian terrace*, built to provide cheap accommodation for the rapidly expanding urban and suburban populations. Still familiar in Britain's towns today, the terraces ranged from the plain, flat-fronted back-to-backs of the factory worker, through various levels of larger, bay-fronted models with classic detailing for the middle classes. Semi-detached and detached *villas*, perhaps with a flourish of Tudor, Gothic or Italianate style, were available for those with more money to spend.

A narrow four-storey Victorian terraced house built in Oxford in 1888.

The many speculative builders of the time felt free to pick and choose and adapt from all the styles of the past, in an age of *eclecticism*. Generally, they tended towards a continued use of the lightweight classical references of Regency until about 1840, turned to the Gothic, Elizabethan and Jacobean styles from about 1850 to 1870, and might dabble in Vernacular Revival, Queen Anne Revival, or a heavy-handed classicism from about 1870 to the turn of the century.

Among the many architect-led trends that developed during the nineteenth century, the most enduringly influential was that of the *Arts and Crafts Movement*. Popular between 1870 and 1930, it returned to pre-Renaissance days for its inspiration, with large, elaborate 'Tudor' chimneys, casement windows, and swooping pitched roofs, and sparked the revival of interest in vernacular styles. The *Art Nouveau* houses of Charles Rennie Mackintosh drew on Scottish vernacular styles, with turrets and rough-cast rendering. His work has a more geometric and austere quality than the ornate Art Nouveau buildings of Europe. A restrained style born of very different sources, was the *Aesthetic Movement*, which combined a rational approach to architecture with the late-nineteenth century taste for all things Japanese.

From the eighteenth century, '*model' villages* and *estates* for workers had begun to appear, built to the taste of wealthy landowners and industrialists, often utilising traditional vernacular styles and designed to be a romantic whole within the surrounding landscape. Among the best-known examples are New Lanark, built by Robert Owen, from the late eighteenth century, and Saltaire, in Yorkshire, which dates from 1850. By the late nineteenth century, this practical form of housing might take the overly nostalgic style of the cottage orné, which could be wildly eccentric with tree trunk supports for porches, fake timber-framing, and thatch so deep it appeared a caricature.

The nineteenth century's increased health problems caused by overcrowding and poor sanitation brought about more widespread concern over poor housing and a growth in rehousing schemes that were eventually to include town *tenements* and *council houses*. As the century closed, there was also a general movement out from town centres towards the suburbs. People became concerned about the house's setting, and out of this grew the *Garden Cities* of Letchworth and Welwyn, and the Garden Suburb of Hampstead.

From the turn of the century until the Second World War, speculative builders created miles of *suburbia* to cater for the taste for fresh air and less crowding. The development of public transport at this time made living out of town a practicable as well as an attractive alternative which was publicised as being a happy and healthy place to live. A London Underground poster of the time

announces 'Golders Green: a place of delightful prospects', and quotes the poem *Sanctuary* by William Cowper. The best schemes were based on the traditional English village and aimed to be complete communities, but there were many more that simply lined the roads into major towns.

Architecturally, many of the houses built have unrelated bits and pieces borrowed from past styles: Gothic Revival windows, Georgian fanlights and timber-frame can be seen adapted and mixed together in some humble semis. The influence of Voysey's brand of vernacular revival is present in the use of pebbledash and porches, their large brick arches sometimes almost circular. Part-glazed front doors might sport stained glass in jazzy colours, or with that popular motif of the thirties, the galleon.

The austere structures of *Modernism*, which came to this country from the mid-1920s, were mildly fashionable, particularly in coastal towns, but were never as popular as the more typical romantic mixes of suburbia. In its purist form, Modernism eschewed ornament: exterior surfaces were painted concrete, kept simple and monochromatic, bays were rejected in favour of large windows in ranks of metal-framed casements. But popular taste, as always, picked out and adopted its favourite parts of this latest style, and softened the look by combining it with vernacular materials. Weatherboarding, tiled or pantiled roofs, and bricks, rather than painted concrete, would be used in colours ranging from pink,

Cottages in Thornton Hough, a village built in the 1890s in Cheshire for W H Lever.

2 5

The Holly Lodge Estate was built in Highgate in the 1920s. The period saw a revival of timber-framing, but used for purely decorative, rather than structural, purposes.

through yellow to brown and, with central heating ensuring comfortable temperatures, large, plain 'picture' windows might be incorporated to give the occupants the maximum view of the world outside.

An early 1930s house designed by W F Crittall, the second son of the founder of the metal window company. The house is not as harshly modern as many examples on the Continent, instead its style is softened by the influence of the Vernacular Revival so popular in the UK at the time.

3

*H*OUSE PLANS

*E*ARLY HOUSE PLANS

Few small houses survive from before the Tudor period. This is not just because of slow deterioration through the centuries, or changing fashions and patterns of settlement. Many early houses were not expected to last more than a lifetime, and were rebuilt for each new generation. However, early structures are still discovered beneath the additions of later centuries: partitioned up, with extra floors inserted, hidden behind Georgian facades, or surrounded by Victorian extensions. So, these house types are not as remote and unrelated to our architectural environment today as they may seem.

The basic plan for early houses was the *hall house*, which comprised just one large, general-purpose, communal living room, open to the roof. It was heated by a central fire blazing on the floor, the smoke escaping through the roof. There were several variations on this theme.

The *long house* had an agricultural emphasis: a byre for animals was attached to one side of the hall and might be as long, sometimes even longer, than the living accommodation for human occupants. Livestock and people shared the same entrance and the byre was not necessarily screened off from the hall. Some long houses could boast small, extra rooms for storage – a pantry for food, and a buttery for drinks. In the *laithe house*, a variation common in Yorkshire, the byre (sometimes combined with a barn) was attached to the house, but completely separated from it by a dividing wall.

The *first-floor hall house*, dating back at least to the time of the Norman Conquest, was built with defence in mind. The ground floor was used for storage or service rooms, while the large hall was

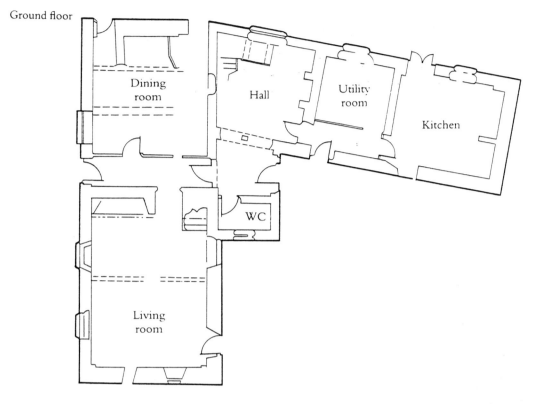

Ground floor

Dining
room

Hall

Utility
room

Kitchen

WC

Living
room

Fifteenth-century Somerset long house with later extensions, including farm outbuildings and a dairy added at an oblique angle. In this plan and those on following pages, room labels show their modern usage, and the layouts include some post-original alterations and additions.

on the first floor and reached by an external staircase. Off the hall, there was usually a 'solar', a small, private room for the owner. Stone-built examples survive from the twelfth century, and this form of house continued to be built until the 1600s in troubled areas such as Cumbria and the Scottish borders, where they were known as 'bastles'.

In the *aisled hall* form of construction, a comparatively wide span could be roofed quite simply, but supporting posts were required inside the building. There is evidence that aisled halls existed in Saxon times, and a number have survived from the later medieval period. In nearly all cases, a floor has been inserted and the supporting posts have been incorporated into later partitions.

In early aisled halls, owner and animals shared the building but, in later examples, the livestock was housed in a separate byre. An extra room, to give the human occupants more privacy, was added, either at ground-floor level or raised to provide storage space beneath. At the other end of the hall, opposite the solar, was the 'screens passage' which protected the hall from draughts and gave access to the service rooms beyond. In early examples, these may have been lean-

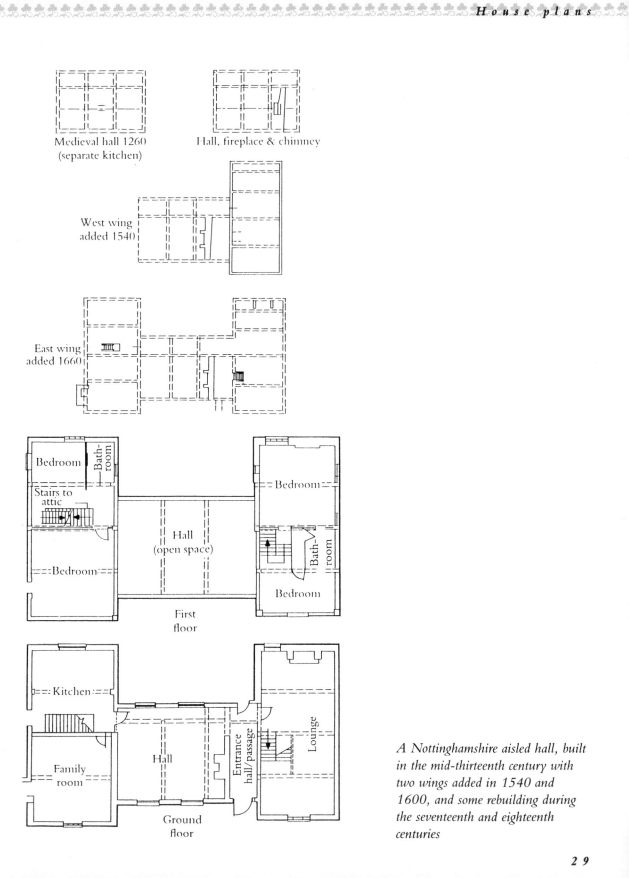

Medieval hall 1260
(separate kitchen)

Hall, fireplace & chimney

West wing
added 1540

East wing
added 1660

Bedroom

Bath-room

Stairs to attic

Bedroom

Hall
(open space)

Bedroom

Bath-room

Bedroom

First
floor

Kitchen

Family
room

Hall

Entrance
hall/passage

Lounge

Ground
floor

A Nottinghamshire aisled hall, built in the mid-thirteenth century with two wings added in 1540 and 1600, and some rebuilding during the seventeenth and eighteenth centuries to structures. The kitchen itself was an independent structure nearby.

With its large, ground-floor hall as the hub of the house, the *medieval manor house* followed the same principles but without the inconvenience of the internal supporting posts. The hall was two storeys high, open to the roof and up to four 'bays' in length – the bay being the space between roof trusses. At one end of the hall were the service rooms, which might be roofed separately or be housed within projecting crosswings. At the other end of the hall was a raised area, or 'dais' where the owner took his meals at the high table. It might perhaps be lit by a large window, sometimes in a bay or 'oriel'. Beyond the dais was the owner's solar.

The *wealden house* is best seen in Kent and West Sussex, where it was usually built to a high standard. Although the wealden house came in a great variety of sizes, its standardised plan appears with only slight variations in different parts of the country. Built from the fourteenth century onwards, its square hall was flanked by two crosswings, often with jettied, or overhanging, upper rooms. Within, the central hall was open to the roof; in the crosswing at one end were a parlour and solar with sleeping room, and at the other end a screens passage, pantry and buttery with either a sleeping room or storage space above them. Cooking was carried out either on a central fire or in a separate building nearby.

Although *town houses* still followed the hall-house principle, their design was often governed by lack of space. The usual town plot was long and narrow, running back from the street, so the hall house was turned side-ways on, with the gable end facing on to the street. The front part of the building was often a shop, and behind this would be the two-storey hall, with offices and stores beyond that. Extra living space might be provided above, and upper storeys on the street façade were usually jettied. Additional storage might be provided by an 'undercroft' or cellar. The kitchen was likely to be a detached structure at the rear, with food carried across a courtyard to the main house.

Alternative town house plans are to be seen where frontage space was wider and the hall could be broadside on to the street, perhaps with a sideway giving access to the rooms at the back. In some cases, the house had two parallel blocks, the rear one possibly used as living quarters.

METAMORPHOSIS

From the fifteenth century, the hall-house pattern started to loose its popularity. The society of the time began to move away from the concept of communal living and towards the privacy provided by separate living quarters. In addition, the Tudor period of prosperity saw a growing desire for ostentation among the wealthy. More money to spend on buildings also meant that they were of better quality, one of the reasons why a higher percentage have survived to the present day.

The *new Tudor design* evolved more to meet higher expectations of comfort than to follow any dramatic changes in fashion and much of the architectural detail remained late medieval. Chimneys were a welcome and major innovation of this time. Central fireplaces had required openings in the roof to allow the smoke to escape, and made upper floors an impossibility. The installation of chimneys made the hall living room a much more pleasant place to be and allowed the construction of first-floor rooms. Previously, the unglazed windows had been kept small, but as glazing too became more common, larger windows became popular.

These changes were not restricted to new buildings: many houses were 'modernised' with bigger window openings, extra floors, partitioned-off rooms and inserted chimneys. Smoke-blackened roof timbers can be evidence that an open hall house has had chimneys added later. The screens passage was a favourite site for a new chimney, perhaps with a newel or spiral staircase installed next to it. Sometimes the screens passage was done away with in favour of a lobby around the door; this allowed two back-to-back fireplaces to be built on to the same stack.

A second chimney might be built in the parlour, which was becoming a more important room, while the hall took on more of the role of a farmhouse kitchen. The parlour might even have its own separate entrance. In long houses, accommodation once allocated to the animals was converted for use by human occupants, the byre might become a kitchen, for example, with a chimney added on the gable wall. Many long-house byres were built to a much lower standard than their halls, and conversion work could often be more a case of rebuilding.

Such changes had their effect on roof structure. Once the open hall lost its popularity, the interiors of roofs were no longer visible and demand for the more decorative forms of internal structure ceased. In addition, existing open hall roofs were altered to give more headroom to newly installed upper floors, and inconvenient tie beams, which ran horizontally across the bottom of the roof's triangle, were often replaced higher up by collar beams, which were supported on braces from the tops of the walls' framing beams.

Because traditional roofing materials required a steep pitch, houses were still one room deep so, to provide more space, extra length, cross wings or lean-to extensions might be added. With such major building work carried out, many a Tudor homeowner took the opportunity to remodel the roof too, perhaps adding dormer windows. So thorough and widespread was this updating of the hall house that it can be difficult to differentiate between a conversion and a new house of this period.

For much of the population in the sixteenth and seventeenth centuries, expensive conversions and elaborate new houses were out of the question. Modest *cottages*, one storey high and with only one room, were numerous but poorly built, and few have survived. The *smaller farmhouses* have fared better. With only two main rooms on each floor, they are sometimes called 'two-unit' houses or, in the north, 'but-and-ben' houses. The rooms were heated either by a central stack, or by a chimney on one or both of the end walls. Basic

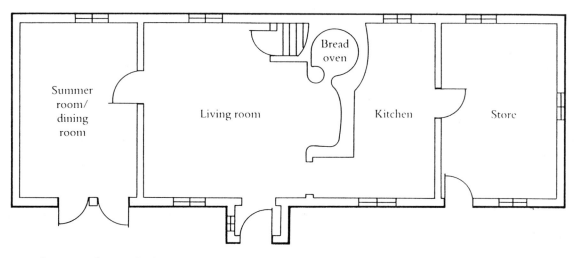

Seventeenth-century farmworker's cottage in south Oxfordshire.

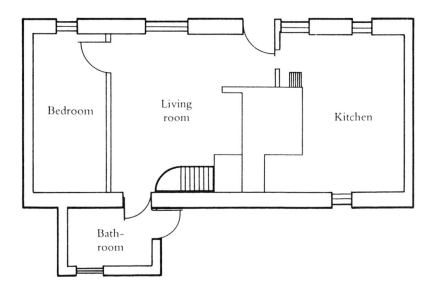

Seventeenth-century farmworker's cottage near Llanidloes, Powys.

rural housing followed this simple traditional design into the nineteenth century, largely uninfluenced by the Renaissance decorative fashions which were affecting the more prosperous. However, such houses did gain a little more space and privacy with the addition of extra small rooms: 'two-and-a-half' and 'two-plus-one' unit houses developed, with the extra accommodation being used as scullery or service areas, and bedrooms – perhaps for servants.

Surprisingly, the period between the late sixteenth and early eighteenth centuries sees the first semi-detached housing. There are examples of two farmhouses built together, possibly to house different generations of the same family. The two halves have sometimes been built at different times, although perhaps only 20 years apart. This idea was taken up and developed in the estate cottages of the late eighteenth century, when 'planned' rural villages, such as Milton Abbas, included semi-detached cottages designed to look like single units.

Like the farmhouses, the changes to *town houses* followed the pursuit of comfort, privacy and space. Narrow town sites restricted the possibilities, but halls could still be floored over, extra storeys

Central portion of a trio of village properties in Essex. It dates from the seventeenth century or before, with various later additions

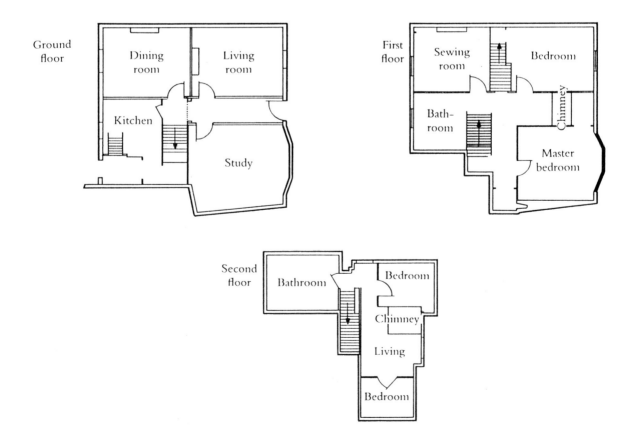

added, and extensions built on at the back. New houses were built with two storeys and, although timber-frame was still often used, both exterior and interior walls were increasingly of brick, or possibly stone. At the top end of the scale, were the well-made, decorative houses of the merchants, while for the poorer town dwellers small, insubstantial terraces were built.

An end-of-terrace cottage, part mid-seventeenth century, part Victorian, in the Darent Valley, Kent.

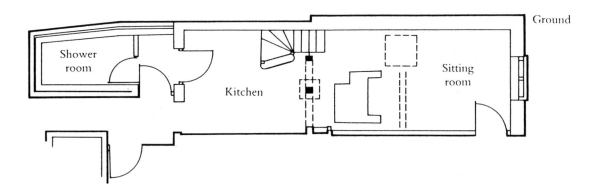

Ground

Shower room

Kitchen

Sitting room

*L*ATE HOUSE PLANS

By the late seventeenth century, the influence of the Renaissance could be seen in the appearance of classical details and a liking for symmetry, a taste which developed first in the towns and then spread to the country. As old houses were enlarged and modified and new ones built, the change in style became apparent: house plans became compact and rectangular, with a symmetrical façade behind which the hall had become an entrance area – sometimes very grand – with the staircase now an important feature.

A Somerset house dating from 1705–15, with Victorian and recent additions.

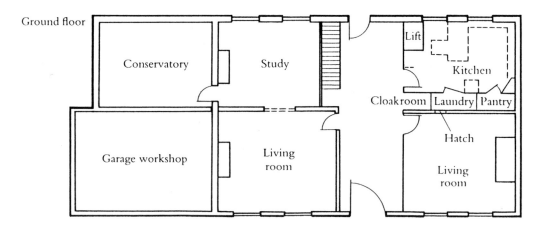

Ground floor

Conservatory

Study

Lift

Kitchen

Cloakroom | Laundry | Pantry

Hatch

Garage workshop

Living room

Living room

Despite the period's wealth, not everyone could afford to rebuild, and many apparently Georgian townhouses are really older buildings refaced, a cheaper way to keep up with the fashion. Behind their formal and symmetrical façades lies the pattern of the old hall house, perhaps with rambling additions.

Although classical features appeared more slowly on country buildings, symmetry became fashionable for *larger farmhouses* during the late seventeenth and early eighteenth centuries. Changes in farming practice brought many prosperity and the opportunity to alter their houses or build new ones. Old farmhouses might be divided up for farmworkers, or modernised, or rebuilt on existing sites. A new Georgian-style house might be built at the front of the plot, with the old farmhouse retained behind it as the kitchen block.

In the new symmetrical plan, the entrance door would open on to a through passage, with rooms of equal size off either side and chimneys in the gable walls. Service rooms were at the rear, often in a single-storey lean-to, with their own separate staircase, cutting down the need to walk through the first-floor rooms. During the seventeenth century, the *single-pile* house (one room deep, perhaps with a lean-to) was superseded by the *double-pile* plan, two rooms deep and two-storeys throughout.

Many *townhouses* were built to much the same pattern as the farmhouses: two rooms deep and three storeys high, they might also incorporate an attic and, perhaps, a cellar. The front rooms might be used for business, with the private ones behind looking out on the garden. The elevation generally had five windows on each of the upper floors, and on the ground floor there were four windows plus a central doorway.

Not all Georgian townhouses were *double-fronted*, however, for where new houses were keeping to the narrow plots of the medieval layout, the *single-fronted* plan had to be adopted. Thus, a common Georgian house plan was the terrace with two rooms, one behind the other, to one side of the entrance hall. Often the ground floor was used for business, with the living rooms on the first floor and the service rooms in the basement, or in a narrow lean-to extension at the back of the house.

Georgian terraced houses spanned a wide cross-section of society, from the fine buildings of Bath to the artisans' homes of east London. But in the nineteenth century, the great increase in the growth of towns resulted in the building of large numbers of cheap terraces, including the back-to-back houses for industrial workers. Although service rooms became more numerous during the nineteenth century, with additions such as wash houses, water closets and coal stores, the plan of the terrace remained largely unaltered, and can still be seen as the basis for a high percentage of our housing today.

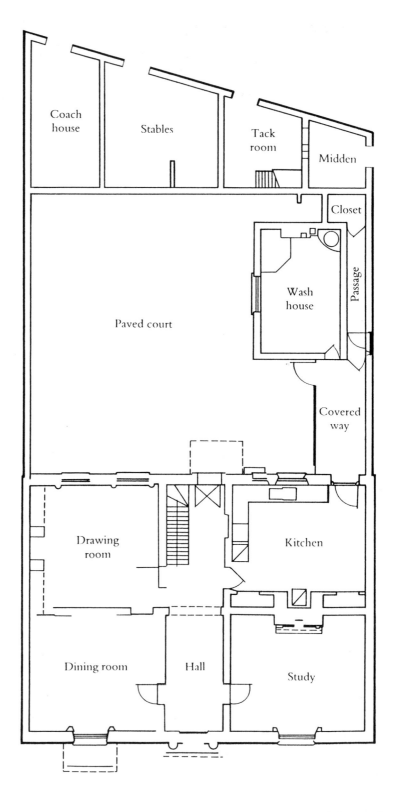

Coach house

Stables

Tack room

Midden

Closet

Paved court

Wash house

Passage

Covered way

Drawing room

Kitchen

Dining room

Hall

Study

Late Georgian two-storey terraced townhouse in Norwich, with extensive outbuildings.

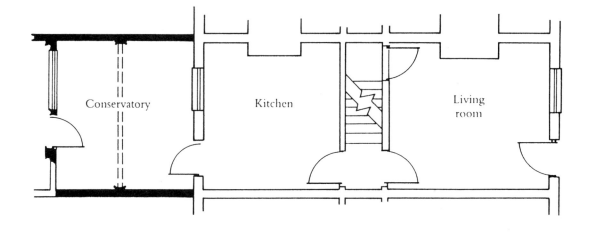

Since Victorian times, terraces have been among the cheapest housing, and better-class housing has comprised the detached and semi-detached. But all three types usually still follow the post-

Late Georgian small terraced townhouse in Surrey.

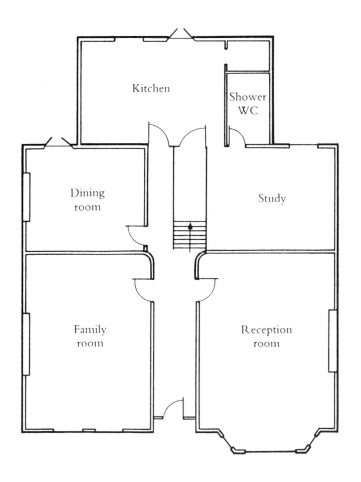

Double-fronted Edwardian townhouse in a London suburb.

Renaissance pattern of regularity, with rooms off an entrance hall and service areas at the rear. Among the differences that have developed, is the accommodation of personal transport. The separate mews buildings of the wealthier Georgians and the sometimes elaborate coach houses of the Victorians have given way to the twentieth century's box-like garages. In many houses from the 1930s onwards, these were adjacent to, or incorporated into, the main building.

The multiple occupancy of one large building has been another development. Nineteenth-century tenement blocks were often built by charitable trusts to replace slums, a course of action pursued again with some of the mid-twentieth century high-rise flats. Smaller-scale blocks of flats have become an accepted part of the housing scene, and often stick less closely to traditional floorplans. From the turn of the century, bungalows too have become popular, although most of those which have not been specially designed conform pretty well to the double-fronted, post-Renaissance floorplan – minus the stairs.

ROOFS

SHAPES

Many early roofs that were once thatched are now tiled or slated, but their original steep pitch, necessary to ensure rainwater ran off before penetrating the thatch, remains as evidence of their past. Indeed, roof shapes have been dictated by prevailing weather conditions, as well as changes in house plan patterns, rather than particular fashions of their own. The plain and practical *gable* has been used throughout the centuries from Land's End to John o'Groats.

Some of the alternatives have been far less successful at throwing off the worst of our wet climate. For example, the central dip of the M-shaped *double-gable* of early double-pile houses quickly clogged up with debris and soon leaked. *Flat* roofs were sometimes used behind the parapets of Georgian houses, and again in twentieth century buildings, but have proved too damp and troublesome to be a long-lasting vogue.

From the time when extra floors were being inserted into open hall houses, the use of roof space has been a concern for builders and homeowners. *Half-hipped* roofs, and gable ends with small windows helped to make the upper floor more useable. But it was the architect, François Mansart (1598-1666), who designed a double-slope roof, the *mansard*, which became a common solution for larger Georgian houses, and the army of staff who slept in the attics. Extra space at the back of the house has often been incorporated under a *catslide* roof, extended from the main roofing at a much shallower angle.

Although fashion largely passed roof shapes by, the decorative

Decoratively curved Dutch gables, favoured during the seventeenth century, on a Suffolk farmhouse.

possibilities of the tops of gable walls has attracted more attention. *Crow-stepped gables* (steps of dressed blocks) were a trend in the early sixteenth century, but they were superseded by *Dutch gables*. Dutch immigrants, many fleeing political and religious oppression, settled in Britain, especially in East Anglia, during the late seventeenth and early eighteenth centuries. The sweeping curves and ogees of gables in their own country were soon introduced and became popular here, the vogue returning, less strongly but over a wider area, as one of the retrospective tastes of the late 1800s.

EARLY ROOF STRUCTURES

Generally speaking, the heavier the timbers used, the older the roof is likely to be. But the shape of rafters can be a clearer guide: until the seventeenth century, common rafters were roughly square in section, or wider than their depth. After this period, they were narrower and deeper. As with the wood used elsewhere in a house, the favourite material until the late seventeenth century was oak, although other native hardwoods were sometimes used, particularly chestnut and elm. From the late seventeenth century onwards, pine and other softwoods were imported from Scandinavia. Early laths or

battens were of oak heartwood and, until the last half of the
nineteenth century, laths were nearly always riven and irregular
rather than sawn and straight.

Unlike roof structures today, tucked away above plastered ceilings,
early houses were open to the roof and the structure was visually
important. Decorative treatments, such as *chamfering* and *moulding*,
indicate that the internal roof structure was meant to be exposed.
Blackened roof timbers can mean that the house was originally an
open hall, with the smoke leaving through the roof rather than a
chimney. Also, the relationship between the roof trusses and the
chimney stacks may show whether they were built at the same time,
or whether the chimneys were later insertions.

Until the late seventeenth century, and in some areas later, roof
trusses were usually made in the carpenter's yard, framed together to
check that they fitted, then taken to pieces again and transported to
the building site. To make sure that the pieces were put together
correctly, they were given *carpenter's marks* – each member was
numbered using Roman numerals. As well as indicating a pre-
eighteenth century building, these marks may also show whether the
house has been lengthened or shortened – or altered (the trusses may
not have been put back in their original order).

There is a complex, sometimes picturesque, vocabulary relating to
early roof structures – do not get bogged down in the jargon. The
terms generally relate to timbers used to stiffen the structure of roofs
designed before the eighteenth century (after that, roofs were
generally much more in today's style, with common rafters and
purlins – horizontal beams that provide intermediate support for the
rafters). The following terms are some of the most frequently used.

The *crown post* rises from a tie beam (running between a pair of
rafters) to support a collar beam further up into the roof's apex.
Crown posts have curved braces and date from the late thirteenth to
the mid-sixteenth century. The building of crown post roofs ceased
when open halls were superseded. Generally, earlier crown posts are
short and thick with four-way bracing; later ones are taller and more
slender, some with only two-way bracing.

From the mid-fifteenth century, the *king post* came into use. A
single, stout and straight upright, this rose from the tie beam, going
all the way up to the roof's apex to support the longitudinal ridge.
As the century progressed, tie beams were installed higher in the
roof's structure, to allow maximum use of attic space, and the king
post became much shorter. *Queen posts* appeared in pairs; vertical or
slightly curved uprights, they rested on the tie beam and supported
the roof's side purlins. King and queen posts are found supporting
roofs over wide, double-pile spans after they had passed out of
common use in smaller houses.

The big curved timbers or 'blades' of *cruck construction* are

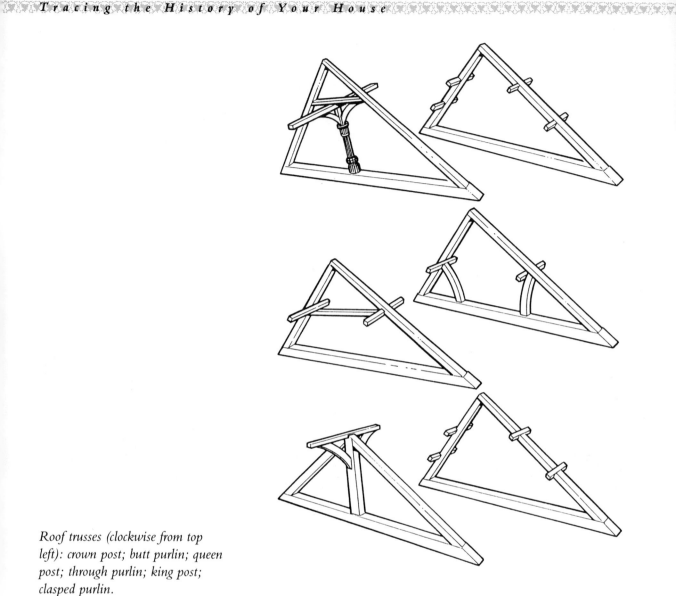

Roof trusses (clockwise from top left): crown post; butt purlin; queen post; through purlin; king post; clasped purlin.

unmistakeable. True crucks, rising from the house's foundations, form a framework for both wall and roof, but they may now be visible only from within the roof, as later extensions to the house, or exterior rendering, often conceal their presence in walls. These impressive structures date from the late fifteenth or early sixteenth centuries. During the 1700s, they were superseded by jointed crucks: these were created from more than one timber, the lower part forming a wall post with the upper piece jointed at an angle to make the roof structure.

The *purlins* of early houses have been the subject of much learned interest, for the form of the joint between the purlin and the roof truss is indicative of several different schools of carpentry. Few of the various types can be pinpointed to exact periods of time, however,

although butt purlins were common from the late sixteenth century to the mid-eighteenth century. Butt purlins are tenon jointed into the principal rafters.

The construction of this Shropshire cottage, with cruck frame set on a base of sandstone, is clearly visible from the side of the building.

MATERIALS

Thatch has been used for roofing in Britian since about 500 BC. Its light weight was ideal for early houses of wattle and daub, and even when clay tiles began to appear in Norman times, it continued to be popular. But thatch has the obvious disadvantage of catching alight easily, and the proximity of thatched houses with the widely-protecting eaves necessary to throw rainwater clear led to a series of disastrous fires in the eleventh and twelfth centuries. As a result, an Ordnance of 1212 prohibited the use of thatch for new roofs in London and existing roofs had to be coated with a fire-proofing daub. Gradually, provincial cities followed London's lead and, as the tile industry started to develop, existing thatched roofs in towns were replaced by tiled ones.

Material	Date									House type
	1500	1550	1600	1650	1700	1750	1800	1850	1900	
Thatch										Large
										Small
										Cottage
Stone										Large
										Small
										Cottage
Tile										Large
										Small
										Cottage
Slate										Large
										Small
										Cottage

Time zones: materials and their principal periods of use for vernacular (i.e. modest) buildings – after Brunskill.

A Devon farmhouse with a typically steeply pitched thatched roof.

The development of the railways during the nineteenth century allowed tiles and Welsh slate, which was then being produced in great quantities, to be easily moved to parts of the country where houses had previously been thatched. At the same time, shortages of labour and materials changed thatch from a cheap roof covering into an expensive one. Although this reduced its use still further, it gave the material snob value and it was used by the wealthy to give a picturesque finish to their country estates and cottages orné. By the beginning of the twentieth century, however, thatching was a dying craft, and it is only in the last 20 years that it has enjoyed something of a renaissance with water reed and wheat straw both in use.

Thatch's fall from favour over the centuries, together with its limited durability, means that there are many houses which were originally thatched, but are now tiled or slated. A steep roof pitch of at least 50 degrees may indicate that the covering was once thatch.

While the history of the plain clay *tile* is not as long as that of thatch, it has still been part of our domestic architecture for many centuries – its dimensions were standardised at 10½ × 6¼ × ⅜ inches as early as 1477. Old tiles are curved so that they arch over the pegs which hold them in place and any sealing material beneath them. Before their production was industrialised in the nineteenth century,

Decorative thatch echoes the patterns of the bargeboards on these revival - style houses in Somerleyton, Suffolk.

The undulating irregularity of hand-made tiles used for roof and wall of a house in Smarden.

tiles were irregular and more textured, with peg holes pierced by punching the wet clay with a stick.

Machine-made tiles are smoother, flatter, and more regular in size and shape but, in reaction against industrialisation, the nineteenth century also saw the reintroduction of Roman-style tiles with protruding nibs to hook over the batten, and the influence of the Arts and Crafts Movement created a market for the rustic-looking reproductions of tiles of earlier centuries.

The curvaceous *pantile* was adopted with enthusiasm in eastern England – probably because of its introduction by the many Huguenot refugees who settled there. Because they do not overlap as much as plain tiles, pantiles are comparatively lightweight, and this made them a good replacement material for roofs that had been thatched and had a less sturdy roof structure. Their lack of overlap also creates a less weatherproof finish, and so they were often torched on the underside with layers of reed and hair-reinforced mortar. The market was served by Dutch imports during the seventeenth century, but in 1701 English manufacture started, and pantiles are still produced.

Laid to a pitch of 30 to 35 degrees, pantiles are usually made from red clays. However, yellow, buff, brown and green clay tiles can also be found, as well as black pantiles, in Norfolk and in Lincolnshire. Eighteenth-century Dutch and nineteenth-century glazed tiles are now particularly rare and valuable.

Natural slate for roofing has been quarried since Roman times, but before the development of the railways in the nineteenth century it was generally only used in the areas where it was mined.

After the nineteenth century's transport revolution, heavy building materials could be moved around the country with ease,

Specially shaped, machine-made roof tiles create a pleasing pattern for this Edwardian house in Shropshire.

Slate roofs at Port Isaac.

and the hard-wearing and non-porous qualities of *Welsh slate* made it a popular covering for the many new houses that were being built for the booming Victorian population. Although that has made it so familiar as a uniform and regular roof covering, Welsh slate had also been used earlier in random widths and thicknesses, giving irregular courses. Other natural slates include: *Lakeland* (blacks and greens), and *Delabole* (dark green, grey, or blue) from the southwest, where it was coated in a cement slurry known locally as 'grouting'.

Stone slates may be called flags, tiles or slates and are made of a variety of different natural materials, including fissile sandstones, limestones and shales. Stone slates tend to be laid gradated, with the largest, heaviest ones at the bottom of the roof slope and the smallest and lightest up near the ridge. The larger sizes tended to be used on simple, low roofs with no fancy work, such as gables, dormers or valleys, and at a pitch of about 30 degrees. In several parts of the country, stone slates are used at eaves' level on roofs covered with other materials, such as clay tile or natural slate.

Both natural and stone slates were often set on a bed of hay, straw or moss and pargeted with shale in lime mortar, and kept in place by hooking a stout peg of animal bone through fixing holes at their head and over laths or battens. Before the nineteenth century,

'ridges' (for the top point of the roof) were often made of long, narrow, suitably carved freestones, but the railways spread the use of Staffordshire clay varieties and solid lead roll ridges.

Although comparatively rare now, wooden *shingles* were utilised as a roof covering up until the eighteenth century. The Romans had used them and they were a popular building material throughout the later Middle Ages. On more substantial houses, they were superseded by clay tiles by the twelfth century.

Artificial tiles can date from as long ago as the mid-nineteenth century, when diamond-shaped cement tiles went into production in Bavaria. But it was the 1930s when 'artifical' roofing materials became more widespread and many modest thirties houses in English suburbs sport concrete tiles and asbestos-reinforced cement tiles, often laid in a diamond pattern.

Artificial Welsh slates and stone slates have recently become available; they tend to have a mechanical appearance and do not weather in the same way as their natural alternatives.

Decorative *bargeboards*, edging the roof, were already in evidence

Stone slate roofs in Burford.

in Tudor times, and they stayed in favour until ousted by the classical taste of Georgian architecture. The nineteenth century's Gothic revival saw them back in the ascendant with their ornamentation becoming increasingly inventive. Even quite humble late-Victorian and Edwardian terraced houses had the flourish of some bargeboarding, perhaps with a touch of Tudor or Gothic style about it. Original bargeboards may bear traces of limewashing but, in their exposed position, they are likely to show the effects of wear. Crisply cut boards are probably from the nineteenth century.

Simple-style scrolls for the bargeboard of a seventeenth-century house in Suffolk.

An intricately detailed bargeboard, probably dating from the nineteenth century, on a seventeenth-century public house in Essex.

*C*HIMNEYS AND CHIMNEY POTS

The comfort of households was greatly increased when an opening in the roof was created over the central hearth, with the interior protected from the weather by a cover or louvre over the smoke hole. Later in the medieval period, fireplaces were improved further with smoke hoods, while in larger houses a smoke bay was formed by partition walls to collect and channel smoke out of the building. The shift of the fireplace to a gable wall with a permanent hood allowed more efficient control of smoke, which could be directed into a smoke chamber where meat was preserved.

As hoods, canopies and flues were usually of lath and plaster on a timber frame, the risk of accidental fire was considerable and a wise fire precaution was to line their interiors with 'parging' or plaster. In 1709 an Act of Parliament required that 'no timber shall lie nearer than 5 inches to any chimney or funnel or fireplace and that all funnels shall be plastered or pargeted on the inside from the bottom to the top'.

It was not until the sixteenth century that chimney stacks first appeared in new, medium-sized and smaller houses and older open halls which were being given a first floor. Stone and brick were both used and, less frequently, cob; sometimes brick was used for a chimney added to an earlier stone building. Some early stacks, particularly in timber-framed houses, projected out from the end gable wall, but later they were generally incorporated into the wall itself.

The towering, though crooked, chimney stack is a proud later addition to a Kent cottage built in 1495.

Early fireplaces burnt large logs and required massive chimneys, but although early stacks were big, they were plain. By the end of the sixteenth century, however, their decorative potential was being exploited, and in all but the most modest of houses elaborate stacks were decorated with specially moulded bricks. Extravagant and individual, the design of the Tudor chimney expressed an extraordinary freedom and inventiveness.

By the late seventeenth century, coal was becoming available; this could be burnt in small grates, so fireplaces and chimneys became smaller. During this period, the influence of the Renaissance also affected design, sometimes in the form of a columnar stacks and classical mouldings, sometimes in a formal symmetry and an increasing plainness. As the Georgian period progressed, the chimney was becoming less and less a feature in itself – leaving the way open for the widespread adoption of the decorative chimney pot.

The idea of adapting chimney tops to help fires draw and to keep out the rain was occasionally applied from about the thirteenth century, but early devices were simple. For example, slits were included in chimneystack sides to allow smoke to escape, or the stack's corners were built up and topped with a flat stone, thus creating four apertures. A more sophisticated alternative was where two stone slates were set up over the chimney opening in the manner of a tent with open ends.

The Tudor period was a golden age for brickwork rather than chimney pots, although the decorative stacks did influence chimney pot design centuries later, and still do so today. Although still rare, there were pots in the sixteenth and seventeenth centuries, and examples exist of open-ended square terminals reminiscent of the tent type of chimney cap, and forerunners of the crown pots beloved by the Victorians.

The Industrial Revolution paved the way for a profusion of pot designs, and during Victoria's reign designs proliferated in a buoyant market. Households of this period had numerous fireplaces using cheap coal and, consequently, a great many chimneys. However, the crowding together of thousands of new houses created downdraughts which caused fires to smoke: extra height for chimney stacks and separate earthenware chimney pots, and metal cowls and chimney extensions were a common solution.

Adorning a mid-nineteenth century house in Bedfordshire, some strongly decorative chimney pots which recall the exuberance of Elizabethan chimneys.

5

WALLING MATERIALS

TIMBER-FRAMING

In areas where good timber was available, wood was used to make the framework for the walls of all but the grandest houses, up until the seventeenth century; however, only a few better-class, well-built, timber-framed houses survive from before the 1300s. By the seventeenth century, the large-scale use of wood for ship building was making timber comparatively scarce. This, combined with the increased production of brick, reduced its use in building, but houses of lighter timber construction continued to be built right through to the nineteenth century.

These later timber-frame houses usually made use of rougher, lighter timbers, which were covered externally with plaster, tiles or weatherboarding. The timber was not intended to be seen, although sometimes it has been exposed since in mistaken restorations. Lightweight timber-framing was often for the houses of the poorer classes, but sometimes it can be found in larger houses, too, in areas where there was little suitable timber.

As with roof timbers, the structure was fitted together at the carpenters, marked up and then reassembled on site. It is the ease with which timber frameworks can be moved which can make them difficult to date, as they can readily be taken down and reused or altered. Mortice holes and notches in illogical places could be an indication that the materials have been salvaged from elsewhere.

Before the sixteenth century, the infill panels were *wattle and daub* (an interwoven basket-type mesh of chestnut, hazel or willow withies covered with clay, chalk and mud). This was finished with lime plaster and limewash, which was sometimes carried over the

(a)

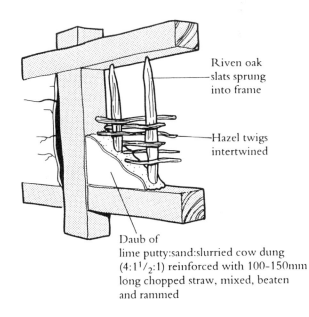

Riven oak slats sprung into frame

Hazel twigs intertwined

Daub of lime putty:sand:slurried cow dung (4:1½:1) reinforced with 100–150mm long chopped straw, mixed, beaten and rammed

(b) Vertical cross section

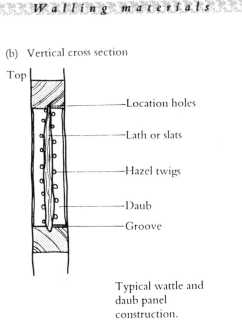

Top

Location holes

Lath or slats

Hazel twigs

Daub

Groove

Typical wattle and daub panel construction.

timbers, and might be tinted with ochre or umber. *Brick infill,* sometimes laid in a herringbone pattern between the timbers, was used for new houses and often replaced wattle and daub in older buildings, from the fifteenth century.

Wattle and daub infill.

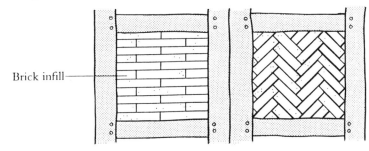

Brick infill

Brick infill patterns.

Where the house was of full *cruck* construction, the curving timbers formed both the wall and the roof structure. Raised crucks, resting on a solid base, might start halfway up the wall and were a useful way of creating space for a second storey after the open hall house became out of date. In *box-framed* houses, the wall timbers were completely vertical.

In early houses, the timbers generally take the form of *large framing,* with panels up to 6 feet square. The panels are strengthened with various forms of diagonal bracing, which might be straight or arched, herring-bone or cross-shaped. *Close studding,* timber-framing with closely spaced vertical studs, generally dates from after about 1500, and was most popular in the well-wooded and affluent south-east of England. The more timber used, the higher the cost of the building work, so close studding was often used as a way to show off wealth and the extra timbers had no structural role to play.

From the mid-fifteenth century, timber in some better-class houses began to be used in *small framing* with panels 2 to 3 feet square. By the seventeenth century, this design had replaced large framing and had spawned *ornamental framing*, an ostentatious fashion which produced spectacularly decorative façades nationwide. All the later timber styles used more wood than large framing and were comparatively expensive, so the same building may have large panelled framing for the less-important parts and more expensive forms at the front.

Simple timber-frame patterns for houses in Pembridge.

Decorative frame patterns on this building in Bridgnorth, Shropshire, include diagonal and ogee strutting and concave side lozenges.

From the mid-fourteenth century, *jettying* appears, its projecting upper storeys providing extra space at first-floor level and giving some weather protection to the ground floor. During the 1400s, jetties became exuberantly decorated and perhaps something of a status symbol. This form of construction continued into the seventeenth century, particularly in towns, although the style became more subdued. In the countryside, jettying became comparatively rare by the end of the sixteenth century.

Some joints, such as the *mortice and tenon,* were used for timber-framing over a long period; others can indicate a more specific date. For example, the *scarf joint* used mirror image cutaways, sometimes highly complex, to attach one piece of wood in line with another and its variations can help date the timber. A less complicated guide to the age of timber-frame, is the use of metal screws, nails, bolts and studs: these did not appear until the sixteenth century; before then wooden pegs were the norm.

*B*RICKS

Brickmaking was introduced into Britain by the Romans; when they left, however, production ceased. Although Saxon and Norman builders could not produce their own bricks, they salvaged and re-used Roman ones, which were only 1½ inches thick and thus looked rather like tiles. Brick production appears to have been beginning once more by the thirteenth century, and there are examples of work in East Anglia apparently made from local clay. These probably mark the reintroduction of brickmaking techniques by immigrant Flemings from the Low Countries. Medieval brickworks and brick kilns are recorded in Hull and along the south coast, where stone and timber were in short supply.

Bricks slowly gained in popularity and by the fifteenth century indigenous production was well underway. But it was the Tudors who heralded a great age for the material, when bricks were shaped by intricate moulds or carved to imitate stone. The narrow Tudor bricks (2 × 9½ × 4⅜ inches) were skilfully used to create spectacular twisting chimneys and highly decorative gables.

From the middle of the sixteenth century, bricks started to be made thicker and the material was being more frequently used for smaller houses. This fashion for brick houses appeared first in the south and east, spreading across the country and gradually replacing timber-framing and cob for the better-class houses, sometimes being used as timber-frame infill in herring-bone patterns and to build chimneys where open halls were being floored over.

Classically based Continental styles arrived in Britain in the seventeenth century, reviving a taste for elaborate brickwork and introducing Flemish Bond, where bricks are laid with each course alternating headers (the ends of bricks) and stretchers (the sides of bricks). The Restoration brought the Court back from the Continent and with them various new ideas on building; the appearance of gauged and rubbed brickwork dates from this time.

Different coloured bricks were used to make decorative patterns, particularly in railway-junction towns which had easy access to the products of other localities. This striking group of houses is in Reading.

Reactions against the use of timber following the Great Fire of London produced a huge demand for bricks: its use as a replacement for infill materials in timber-frame and for building chimneys accelerated, and it was also popular as quoins (the external corners of a wall) and dressings (to doors and windows) for houses being built of cheaper materials. By the late seventeenth century, smaller houses were quite commonly of brick and, by the eighteenth century, it had become the most usual material for these buildings.

Many timber and cob houses were refaced with brick during this time, in pursuit of a more formal look. The first brick tax, introduced in 1784, dealt brick's popularity a blow, and the Regency period saw stone superseding it as the most fashionable building material. However, bricks (often of poor quality) were still used behind those façades which were designed to be covered with stucco, and they re-emerged as the dominant building material as Victorian morality found the imitative nature of stucco 'dishonest'.

From the sixteenth to the early eighteenth century, red brick was popular, but by the mid-1700s, Georgian taste reacted against red, and bricks were required to imitate the colours of stone. Grey, brown, buff and yellow bricks were being used, generally with red dressings and quoins. In London, the well-known yellow 'Stock' became almost universal, but by the second half of the nineteenth century, it began to acquire a working-class image, and red bricks came back into favour for better-class houses. Buildings displaying brickwork of two or more different colours are to be found after the development of the railways facilitated and transportation of bricks; it occurs particularly in towns that had important junction stations, such as Crewe and Reading, where multi-coloured brickwork was used to highly decorative effect in the late Victorian period.

By the mid-nineteenth century, machine-made bricks were taking over from the handmade, except for the best-quality work. Smoother and more regular in appearance, machine-made bricks are easy to differentiate from older examples, but the rustic quality of handmade bricks has been championed by the Arts and Crafts' vernacular revival and some of the cottage-style building during this century.

Brick sizes and bonds (the patterns in which they are laid) have also changed over the centuries and can be a more specific guide to dating than changes in taste. An act of Parliament of 1776 fixed the size of bricks to be used throughout the country at $8\frac{1}{2} \times 4 \times 2\frac{1}{2}$ inches. After 1784, when the first brick tax was introduced, larger bricks were made (the tax was calculated on numbers of bricks). Some bricks of this period were as large as $10 \times 5 \times 3$ inches. In 1803, a further tax was levied against these large bricks, and this was avoided by reducing their size to $9 \times 4\frac{1}{2} \times 3$ inches. The brick tax was removed in 1850, and since then the size of the brick has been largely standardised, rising four courses to a foot. In the north of England, however, larger bricks, rising four courses to 13 inches, were used for much of the nineteenth century. The Standard British size for bricks was metricised in the 1960s to $65 \times 215 \times 102.55$ mm.

In early brick buildings the bonding is often irregular, but English bond, with alternating rows of headers and stretchers, became usual by the end of the sixteenth century. Flemish Bond, with alternate headers and stretchers in each row, was introduced in the seventeenth century, and had largely replaced English Bond by the early 1700s. In some places, Header Bond was popular in the eighteenth century, with dark headers sometimes used to form ornamental patterns. The 1800s saw the development of cavity walls, where two leaves of wall were held together only by metal ties. As header bricks were no longer needed to link the two leaves together, Stretcher Bond gradually became widespread.

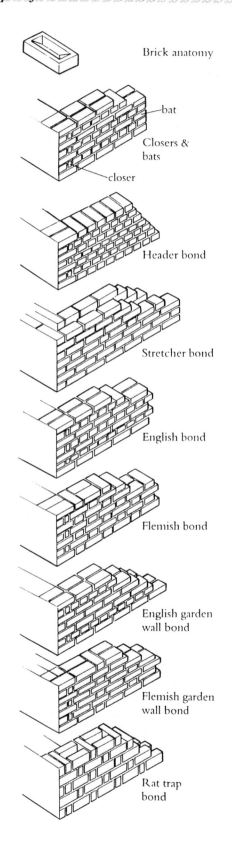

Brick anatomy

bat

Closers & bats

closer

Header bond

Stretcher bond

English bond

Flemish bond

English garden wall bond

Flemish garden wall bond

Rat trap bond

COB

Raw clay is a universal building material, and it was used throughout the British Isles for humble homes – and occasionally for larger ones, too. Clay as a building material has a variety of recipes and names including cob, shilf, clom, wychert, clay lump and clay bat. It was used particularly in areas where there was an inadequate supply of timber, but the best and most durable buildings are to be found in chalk areas, particularly Devon. The nature of the material means that neat angular corners are impossible, so these were either rounded off or given quoins of another material; sometimes gable ends were built in rubble. Cob walls are thick and often built tapering (to a batter).

Cob's characteristic rounded corners and rough surface for a Devonshire cottage.

Clay houses were recorded in London and Devon during the thirteenth century, but those that survive are more likely to date from the late eighteenth and nineteenth centuries. Although many examples have been lost, some possibly still remain undiscovered, for the material demands a waterproof covering and sometimes hides behind a layer of mathematical tiles (see page 62), or bricks. Older cob houses were usually plastered and lime washed. The material also requires a firm foundation base of stone, flint or brick. Dating cob is difficult and best considered in relation to other characteristics, in particular the materials used in the wall base may give a clue – stone and flint being earlier than brick.

61

CLADDING

A decaying Devon barn reveals its cob structure combined with stone buttresses.

Mathematical tiles are fixed vertically to walls and give a very convincing appearance of brickwork. They were popular during the eighteenth and nineteenth centuries, when they were used to clad both old and new buildings, particularly in the south-east, where good building stone was scarce. Although it has been suggested that they may have been seen as a way to avoid paying brick tax (which was levied between 1784 and 1850), they were in use both before and after that time. Also, for part of that period, the tax was levied on tiles, too, and for a number of years tiles were even taxed at a higher rate than bricks.

Their popularity seems more likely to be because they could waterproof a building, or hide an unfashionable façade. Early mathematical tiles were often a shade of red, although this depends on local clays, but as Georgian taste turned from red brick towards stone, stucco or stone colours, mathematical tiles followed the trend with greys, browns and yellows.

Although the tiles varied slightly, they were made brick-shaped, and the range included half or quarter lengths which would look like headers so that brick bonds could be imitated. Where the tiles are over brick or stone buildings, they are attached with mortar; where they cover a timber-frame building they are either nailed on, or mortared, or both. Mathematical tiles are often assumed to be brickwork until the nails or bedding fails, and it is only around details, such as windows, that the deception may become obvious.

Mathematical tiling was fashionable in towns, *weatherboarding,* the use of wooden planks as a cladding material, was perhaps its rural, and poorer, equivalent. Again popular in the south-east, its use is

Weatherboarding gives a classical veneer to this Georgian-style house in Cranbrook.

One of Kent's many tile-hung cottages.

Randomly laid Horderley Sandstone.

believed to have started at about the same time as tiling, and there is the same sort of dispute about whether it was a reaction to the brick tax. Like mathematical tiles, it offered an extra protective coat against the weather and perhaps a simpler, more fashionable, façade than the outmoded timber-frame. In the wooded lands of Kent, the look of weatherboarding seems to have been particularly appreciated, for it was used to give a classical veneer to the houses of the comfortably off.

Boards of oak and elm were first used on farm buildings. Oak was the favourite wood, and when elm was used it tended to be in wide planks, sometimes with the exposed edge unsawn ('waney-edged') to help guard against rot. By the mid-seventeenth century, softwood was being imported and, during the later years of the eighteenth century, power saws were ensuring a ready supply of uniformly finished wood for cladding houses.

Tile hanging belongs in this cladding family, too, and shares characteristics of time and place: it was popular in the south-east, particularly Kent, between the late eighteenth and mid-nineteenth centuries, although it had been in use from about 1690. The tiles were either hung on nails or had lugs which were hooked over laths, and were sometimes used to clad lightweight upper storeys of a house with a brick-built ground floor. Although plain roofing tiles were commonly used, decorative effects were achieved with specially-shaped tiles and by combining different colours.

STONE

The use of stone for houses relates more to geography than history. In areas where stone was readily available from shallow quarries, or could be scavenged from demolished buildings, it was used, often in a pretty rough form, from earliest times. Re-use of stone was also common, so although it may bear mason's marks, these are not always a foolproof clue to the age of the house of which it is currently a part. Stone houses survive from medieval times but, as with early buildings of other materials, they are usually the substantial and well-built examples, such as manor houses and merchants' houses, better able to withstand the passage of time.

From the seventeenth century, stone became more fashionable under the influence of the Renaissance and was more likely to be used in parts of the country where it was not indigenous, though this remained a prerogative of the wealthy. By this time, there was a tradition of high-quality masonry work in areas blessed with a good building stone, such as the Cotswolds, where it was used for quite modest houses.

Ashlar stone, with its smooth finish and squared shape, was more expensive than rubble and used in better-class buildings. It had

particular appeal for classical façades. Rusticated stone, in which an indented pattern rather like worm holes has been chiselled, was also used for classical and revival buildings from the 1600s through to the twentieth century.

Stone buildings often have brickwork door and window surrounds and quoins, and the bricks may help to date the building. From the late eighteenth century onwards, stone finishes were simulated by materials such as Coade stone, stucco, plaster and, most recently, cement.

Until the eighteenth century, limewash was commonly used as an external covering for rubble walling, and sometimes even for ashlar too, to help improve its weather resistance. Bare stone became fashionable in the 1800s and many older stone houses had their limewash removed at that time, but the substance is difficult to remove completely and you may still be able to find some traces.

A smooth 'dressed' finish for Hoar Edge Grit stone, in this early seventeenth-century Shropshire house.

*Limestone cottages with brick lintels,
at Much Wenlock, Shropshire.*

FLINT

Generally used in areas where it was most easily available, flint has a highly decorative tradition in Norfolk where it has been used for building since Roman times. Cobble buildings usually combine other building materials for the dressings, as corners and openings for doors and windows cannot be formed by irregular flints. Earlier examples make use of stone but, by the seventeenth century, brick was being used. Often the type and colour of these bricks will be a better clue to the age of the building than the cobbles themselves which, as a natural material, remain timeless.

Knapped flint, where the stone was split to give a flatter surface, required more work and was found in buildings of better class. Sometimes flints, whether knapped or not, are interleaved with alternate bands, chequerboard or diaper patterns in brickwork. This is partly to strengthen the wall, but partly for decoration and, occasionally, includes a date clumsily picked out on the wall surface in brick.

Although the types of flint vary from the rough angular ones gathered from fields to cobbles washed smooth by sea and rivers, their use is governed by availability rather than changing fashions. Indeed, the use of flint as a building material in East Anglia is a tradition which continues to this day.

ℛENDERING

Wattle and daub, intertwined vertical and horizontal sticks covered with daub, were used for both internal and external walls from earliest times – the ancient Egyptians used the same system. The daub, which was a mix of earth and sand, cow dung and straw, had to be moist but firm. It was pushed into the wattle framework, which consisted of cleft oak, ash or alder uprights and withies of hazel, cleft oak, chestnut or beech, used unseasoned so that they remained malleable. Progressively weaker layers would be used and the top surface was limewashed.

As wattle gave way to sawn and riven laths, daub gave way in most areas of the country to *clay/lime* and *lime plaster* mixes. Lime was initially produced on a small scale and made use of on more formal projects and for mortar between stones. It was also used to give a thin render to random rubble walls to improve their appearance and give them better weather resistance. In fourteenth-century London, it was used for fireproofing and applied to chimneys and thatch on high-risk buildings to comply with a City ordinance. It was also applied to timber-frame buildings – sometimes between the frame members but in the south-east usually across both wood and wattle.

Flint, with brick dressings for a farmhouse near Eastbourne.

From the sixteenth to the late seventeenth century, decorative panels known as *pargeting* became popular across the south and east in a line extending from Devon to York. The ornamentation was incised, pressed and moulded on to a render made from a variety of recipes, and appears on houses that were either timber-framed or made of clay lump. Early pargeting uses geometrical patterns and panels depicting flowers, animals, figures and coats of arms. Later designs show a classical influence. Combs were often used to create patterns on early pargeting, while later designs were made using timber moulds.

Stamped work, a Victorian equivalent to pargeting, is to be found on many urban buildings. It relied on a hard mix of Portland cement with the pattern stamped out in decorative panels.

After the Renaissance, architects revived Roman recipes for coatings which could hardly be distinguished from stone. In England, from as early as 1500, various kinds of render were used in non-stone areas to simulate stone dressings but, despite the changing aspirations of its users, the mixture still contained the traditional ingredient, lime. During the eighteenth century, there were numerous attempts to develop a more durable substitute for lime-based renderings, and a series of recipes were patented from 1713 to 1815; they included some bizarre ingredients, ranging from brown sugar to powdered glass. Initial recipes were known as 'oil mastics' and were used as an overall facing and for decorative ornamentation.

In 1796, Parker's *cement* was registered, its manufacture involving firing stone fragments at such a high temperature that they became almost vitrified. This was the first step in changing the character of rendering material, but it was still a natural product rather than a man-made one. Attempts to produce a similar, but artificially made material, resulted in the first patent for Portland being registered in 1824. Strong and rapid-setting, its use was quickly taken up by many builders and architects, and a number of alternatives were available by the middle of the century.

From 1810 to 1850, *stucco*, the use of a render to give the appearance of stonework, was tremendously fashionable, but in the second half of the century its popularity started to wane. It was thought to look cheap, and offended the new advocates of honesty of materials. However, rendering continued to be used through Victorian times, although the quality of workmanship declined during the period of mass speculative building. As the nineteenth century progressed, it lost popularity in favour of terracotta, Coade stone and Portland stone.

The artificial stone known as *Coade stone* was first produced in the late eighteenth century by a company run by Mrs Eleanor Coade. It was well-made and frost resistant, and its popularity was given a boost by the 1774 Building Act which banned the use of exposed

woodwork for window frames, porches and cornices. Items available in Coade stone ranged from 9 foot high models of river gods to keystones, chimney tops and friezes decorated with laurel patterns. Although easily mistaken for real stone, it is actually a form of terracotta which is moulded and fired in a kiln.

Roughcast, rendering combined with stone aggregate, was in use in the north and west of England before 1850, and was soon widespread throughout the country as its application required relatively little craftsmanship. It was useful to give a flat, waterproof surface to weaker or irregular materials. Its distinctive texture is achieved by throwing the mix at the walls, and later versions are distinguished by the less varied effect achieved by mechanical throwing techniques.

Terracotta details in a late nineteenth-century house match perfectly with the colour of the brickwork.

6

*D*OORS AND WINDOWS

*E*ARLY MULLIONED AND CASEMENT WINDOWS

Up until the sixteenth century, the windows of smaller houses were unglazed and fitted with internal shutters. The window design was square headed and divided vertically by timber uprights, or mullions, square in section, but set diagonally. This form continued to be used for poor houses and less-important rooms well into the seventeenth century, but better-class houses' windows were increasingly glazed. The mullions were usually of stone, and sometimes they had a Gothic-style arch.

By the mid-sixteenth century, glass was being used in windows in the form of small panes linked by lead strips, or cames, which were flexible enough to cope with the irregularities of early glass. A vertical iron bar, a saddle bar, might be riveted to the centre of the window frame so that the soft lead framework could be tied to it to prevent sagging. Many early leaded windows, or lights, were fixed and did not open, but opening casements were usually strengthened with iron surrounds.

Mullion design gradually changed from a straight splay to one that was slightly hollowed and, by the late seventeenth century, there were also other shapes current: a convex moulding with square fillets at the angles and a plain square section. Windows generally remained long, low and horizontal until the mid-seventeenth century, when the influence of the Renaissance started to make itself felt. Then the windows of larger houses started to be taller, narrower, and often only two lights wide. To cope with this new

Early windows, with characteristic narrow wooden mullions, from the Little Hall in Lavenham, Suffolk.

Supporting saddle bars are visible in the windows of a Surrey farmhouse dating from about 1660.

A sixteenth-century house in Essex displays both square and diamond panes.

height, a horizontal member, a transom, was added, forming a cross with the vertical mullion.

The sash window started to displace the popularity of casements during the early eighteenth century, but they continued to be installed, although at a much reduced level, with larger glass panes in a timber framework now the norm. To cater for the retrospective tastes of the early nineteenth century, cast-iron casements were divided into small panes and looked similar to leaded lights, while the Vernacular Revival styles of the 1930s saw a further vogue for small panes, surrounded by leading and set into a timber surround. During the 1920s and 1930s, the Modern movement precipitated a widespread use of simpler, metal-framed casements.

*Leaded glass and an oriel shape –
Queen Anne revival style for a
Hampstead house of 1895.*

*The mid-nineteenth-century
windows of a Suffolk village school
show complex lattice patterns
reminiscent of early leaded lights.*

7 3

Sash Windows

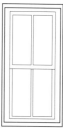

In all but the grandest houses, early sash windows (dating from the end of the seventeenth century) had numerous panes and thick glazing bars.

As the sash window developed and grew popular during the eighteenth century, more slender glazing bars and the 'six-over-six' pattern of panes evolved.

As mass-produced glass became available from 1838, the four-over-four design became popular, followed by the two-over-two configuration (below) and finally, the one-over-one design (bottom).

Sash windows are believed to have been developed in Britain in about 1670 and were quickly adopted, not only because they admitted more light, but also because they suited classically derived styles of Queen Anne and Georgian houses. Windows other than double-hung timber sashes were seldom used for buildings of consequence from 1700 onwards and, during the early years of the eighteenth century, many existing casement windows were modified or exchanged for them.

In the smaller houses at this time, however, old mullioned windows were sometimes replaced by side-hung casements, or by horizontally sliding sashes. Both of these were cheaper than vertically sliding sashes, and suited the horizontal window openings typical of such houses.

The appearance of the sash window has altered considerably through the centuries. The earliest types had 20 or more small panes of glass, and the glazing bars could be over 2 inches thick. But sash window design developed quickly towards the use of fewer, larger panes of glass with more slender glazing bars, and by about 1700 the six-over-six type (with six panes of glass in each sash) was becoming common.

It remained widespread for the next 150 years, but variations in glazing patterns appeared by the late eighteenth century, with Gothic designs, or slender glazing bars made of iron or brass, but painted to look like wood, being other options. A common design by the early nineteenth century had fairly large panes in the centre of each sash, bordered with narrow panes. By the mid-nineteenth century, the availability of sheet glass was having a great effect on the design of sash windows. At first, four-over-four arrangements (with each sash carrying four panes of glass) became common, then two-over-two and, finally, each sash was filled by a single large pane. Many earlier windows had their glazing bars removed at this time.

While these changes in design allowed in more light, without vertical glazing bars to brace them, Victorian sash windows were much less robust. To give added strength, brackets or 'horns' were used to extend the vertical stiles below the bottom rail of the top half of the window. This feature is common in sash windows after 1838.

The sash window's design revolution took place despite the imposition of window tax in 1696 and excise duty on glass in 1746, costs which were increased until 1825 and not abolished until 1851. To lessen the financial burden, many windows were blocked up and the results can still be seen in many old houses today. Not all blocked windows are the result of taxation, of course; they may simply have been necessitated by internal replanning. Others were always false

The evolution of sash window styles.

but included to provide the symmetry demanded by eighteenth-century taste; they were sometimes painted to look like actual windows. Unlike later alterations, the infilling in these blind windows would be recessed, although generally bonded into the surrounding walling.

Changes in building regulations may also give clues as to a window's age, although these are more reliable for houses in the London area than for the provinces, where official recommendations were not always put into practice. Before 1709, sash boxes were usually mounted pretty well flush with the surrounding masonry. But concern about fire risks led to the requirement that sash windows of London houses be recessed 4 inches back from the masonry. In 1744, this law was extended so that sash boxes not only had to be recessed inwards, but also sideways behind the masonry itself, thus leaving just a narrow strip of wood exposed on either side.

The mechanics of the sash window have changed little compared with its stylistic developments. In the earliest examples, the lower half of the window was fixed and the upper sash was not always hung on cords and weights; wooden stops in the frame prevented the sash opening beyond a certain point. Over a hundred years later, the heavy, full-height sash windows of Victorian dwellings often employed chains rather than cords. In this century, some sash windows were 'improved' by the removal of the sash cords, weights and pulleys in favour of spiral sash balances, and a recent alternative is the adjustable spring tape balance (like a coiled-spring tape measure) which has been used with very light sashes.

$\mathcal{O}$LD GLASS

Despite its fragility, old glass does survive and it can be a useful guide to whether a window is an original or a reproduction. Old glass is much less regular than that produced since the perfection of sheet glass in the mid-nineteenth century, and it is quite likely to have air bubbles, perhaps a slight tint and to produce distortions. Curved glass was made for Georgian bow windows and in Victorian times, too, but is rarely made today. Modern glass is mostly either completely flat and uniform, or attempts to reproduce a period look with exaggerated textures and colours. Bottle, or bull's eye, glass is a favourite for this treatment: in the past it was considered a waste product and only used in the cheapest of houses or the least important rooms. Situated in a prominent position, such glass is more likely to be a modern version.

SHUTTERS AND FIXINGS

Internal shutters continued to be used even after glazed windows became widespread. Early examples were of plain oak, but they progressed to the panelled folding ones typical of Georgian times, while vertical sliding shutters are sometimes found dating from the late eighteenth and nineteenth centuries.

Original fastenings may have survived along with their windows: those for early wrought-iron casements would have been made by the local blacksmith, and other similar examples may be found in the same area. Early iron casements with wood surrounds were sometimes hinged in the modern way, but more often they were hung on pins in the frame, the system used for stone surrounds.

DECORATIVE SURROUNDS

During the sixteenth and seventeenth centuries, decorative 'hood' or weather moulds on the exterior wall above windows protected them from rainwater. By the end of this period, separate hood moulds were being superseded by one continuous moulding over all adjoining windows. Slowly, this moulding changed into a continuous string course, marking the storey heights, and in the eighteenth century the final stage of its development can often be seen as a projecting band of brickwork at the various upper floor levels.

Window surrounds in brick houses of the seventeenth and early eighteenth centuries were often decorated with contrasting brick dressings, and their arches given projecting, perhaps carved, keystones. As the eighteenth century progressed, simpler façades were preferred and these features became less common.

FANLIGHTS

Overdoor lights became common as the layout of the ordinary terraced house evolved into the form we know today: the front door opening on to a narrow passage leading to a wider staircase compartment. In this plan, an overdoor was pretty well a necessity, and became more so as the development of back additions reduced the light available from the rear. In large houses, there was sometimes a fanlight in a second door which formed a draught lobby behind the outer street entrance.

At first, most overdoors were simply rectangular, and there is little evidence of decorative glazing. But an illustration published in 1725 shows a decorative fanlight, semi-circular and with fretted radiating panels. From about that date, the fashion for fanlights spread as the new classical style of architecture was popularised by architectural pattern books. The vogue was not limited to new houses, and many existing ones had later fanlights inserted into their doorcases.

A wooden fanlight of the 1720s, within a doorcase in Hampstead, London.

A typical fanlight would be semi-circular and made in timber with a glazing pattern similar to a round-headed window but with added festoons. The glazing bars would have their moulded sides facing the street, where they would be seen to the best advantage.

Timber fanlights continued to be made in this style, especially in rural areas, throughout the eighteenth and early nineteenth centuries, but around 1760 they began to be displaced by more fanciful designs made of metal.

A fine fanlight in a Georgian doorway in Dublin's Merrion Square, which was built from 1762.

As early as the 1740s, experiments had begun in the use of metal glazing bars and, eventually, a compound wrought iron and lead glazing bar was invented, removing the need for carving. By 1780, lead was the most commonly used fanlight material in London, and it continued to be so until the end of the eighteenth century. Other materials in use during the 1770s included 'compo' (a composition made largely of chalk, animal glue and linseed oil), which was used to create ornaments for timber fanlights.

The early years of the nineteenth century saw a change in the style of fanlights. Although radiating designs continued to be produced, they were less ornate, often with curved glazing bars and only a minimum of applied ornament. Sometimes they featured a central circle where the house number could be added, or a lantern set. In some examples, the central circles were even pivot-hung for ventilation.

The new town terraces of the 1820s displayed thousands of pretty fanlights, mostly with 'teardrop' or 'batswing' patterns, but also some unusual designs. Although such fanlights continued to be a feature through to the 1840s, for urban houses their popularity declined, partly due to the introduction of cheap plate glass in 1838. In less fashionable areas of the country, fanlights persisted much longer.

A late eighteenth-century fanlight incorporates a lantern fitting.

DORMERS AND SKYLIGHTS

Dormers (constructions with a gable roof and a window that projects from a sloping roof) have been incorporated in houses since the sixteenth century, but their use falls into three main phases. When the open hall houses of medieval times were floored over to provide a second storey, dormers were used to light the rooms created in the roof space. Even new houses built at this time followed the same pattern and had prominent dormers. The next phase resulted from the architectural changes of the Renaissance, when servants' bedrooms were often in the steeply sloping roofs of the tall, compact Georgian houses. The third vogue for dormers was during the struggle for healthier living conditions following the epidemics of such diseases as cholera during the nineteenth century. Dark, unventilated spaces were deplored and legislation evolved to prescribe window areas.

Skylights were used mainly from the eighteenth century to light cottage bedrooms, storerooms or corridors. Following the changes in regulations since the nineteenth century, many earlier skylights were considered inadequate and were replaced by dormers.

Although the design of dormers changes regionally, they have a general tendency to look 'old-fashioned' in comparison with a house's other windows. In addition, the dormer has played its part in revival styles at various times: imitations of sixteenth-century houses 'modernised' with dormer windows were built in the 1800s; Queen Anne revival houses include decorative Dutch-style dormers, and the Vernacular Revival houses of the turn of the century copied the dormers of the 1600s and 1700s.

BOW AND BAY WINDOWS

The projecting window has been appreciated by the British for the last 500 years. Large bay windows lit the dais end of the fourteenth-century hall houses, and by the fifteenth century there was a variety of decorative designs. Bays remained an important architectural feature of Elizabethan and Jacobean houses, and continued to be used in the brick and timber-framed houses of the gentry and prosperous farmers throughout the seventeenth century. They were, however, too expensive to be used in most vernacular buildings, although in the limestone belt which runs from Northamptonshire to Dorset, they did appear in small village houses after about 1660.

For the polite, formal houses built from the middle of the seventeenth century, the bay was considered unsuitable, and it was not until there was a relaxation of adherence to strictly classical design that bays started to regain popularity. By the middle of the

Oriel windows in Smithfield London. They predate the Great Fire of 1666.

eighteenth century, they were being used to enliven country houses and add informality to urban villas. These bays were substantial, with classical proportions, and visually linked to the rest of the house perhaps by a contrasting string course, a moulded cornice or continuous parapet. As the century progressed, scaled-down versions appeared on smaller houses. The window tax, introduced in 1696, may have encouraged shallow bow windows, a style which was used for shop fronts from 1750.

Semi-circular bays, usually in pairs on a street location, remained popular into the nineteenth century, but a building Act in London prohibited the projection of domestic windows beyond the general frontage of the rest of the house. Shop windows' projection was limited to 10 inches. Although discouraged in London, projecting windows continued to be popular elsewhere, particularly at seaside resorts.

The bow window of a Gloucestershire house, which was probably once a shop.

By the mid-nineteenth century, however, the curved shape gave way to a more angular one and saw the influence of the popular revival styles. The window tax was repealled in 1851, and simple, square bays appeared on urban terraces, relieving their monotony. More and more elaborate embellishments were developed, and the windows grew larger to light the terraces' long, narrow rooms. In 1878, a building act limited the bays' projection to less than 3 feet, and its size to no more than three-fifths of a house's total frontage. The bay's most recent development was to follow the influence of the Vernacular Revival style, with the cosy tile-hung or timber-frame examples to be seen in the urban housing of the 1930s.

STAINED GLASS

Until the nineteenth century, stained glass was rarely found in private houses. Then, with the Gothic revival and the enthusiasm of the designer/architect Augustus Pugin, it captured the attention of the colour-loving Victorians, became the norm for front doors of even modest terraced houses, and was set into windows for passages and halls. Demand grew until about 1870, after which it tailed off slowly, with the galleon and sun designs of the 1930s proving to be its swan song.

Before the nineteenth century, stained glass was limited to the most important rooms of grand houses, where heraldic motifs were often used, as in this Elizabethan house in Dorset.

Stained glass provides privacy and decoration for a North London Edwardian terraced house.

Stained glass for both the porch gable and the door itself in an 1890s house in South London.

A great deal of stained glass has been removed, either because it was damaged, or because it was so alien to post-war taste. In the past few years, there has been more interest in this decorative form, and new or replacement stained-glass windows and doorlights have been inserted in old properties. Checking the design against those of neighbouring houses may indicate whether stained glass is original or not.

DOORS

Simple planked doors were used for the main entrances of ordinary houses from the Middle Ages, and continued to be the norm until the late seventeenth century. Indeed, the planked door remained common for modest houses and for the servants' rooms of grander ones until the late nineteenth century – more than 100 years after the panelled door had taken its place in all positions of importance.

The planked door is very similar to that of the modern garden shed: ledged, but rarely braced and framed. But front doors of this kind were made of oak and the planks were wedge-shape in section, having been cut radially from a log to reduce warping. The thin edge of each one was tucked into a small slot or rebate cut in the thick edge of its neighbour to achieve a draught-proof form of construction, presenting a smooth surface on the inner, ledged, side of the door, but a serrated one to the outer side. Braces, if fitted, were seldom morticed into the ledges but, instead, butted into shallow angle recesses.

Throughout the several hundred years of its reign, the planked front door changed relatively little in design, making individual examples difficult to date. However, a little before the end of the seventeenth century, flat planks of baltic pine replaced wedge-shaped planks of oak.

PANELLED DOORS

Simple planked doors were not the only type to be used in the fourteenth, fifteenth and sixteenth centuries. More elaborate panelled doors were not only made for grand buildings such as large manor houses, castles and churches, but also were occasionally found in quite modest buildings, such as farmhouses.

Although smaller and simpler houses continued to have vertical planked doors, by the end of the seventeenth century the influence of the Renaissance was affecting door design, via architectural pattern books. In the houses of more sophisticated design, panelled doors were often used, with four or six panels, often moulded and sometimes with raised panels.

This change now appears an abrupt one but there are a few examples of 'interim' forms: early Queen Anne front doors could sometimes be quite elaborate and composed of eight or more panels with hints of both the Stuart tradition and the up-and-coming classicism. Sometimes they were also transitional in a different way: on the outer side they had formal panels and mouldings presenting a grand and dignified face to the world, while a simple planked inner face was adequate where show was less important.

By the early 1740s, however, the typical front door had evolved into a new and more or less standard form, which it was to retain for about the next century, although there were numerous variations on the theme. Nevertheless, the six-panelled Queen Anne or Georgian door, which can still be seen gracing hundreds of thousands of houses all over Britain, was by far the most common.

Often, though not always, the proportions were 'double square', its height being twice its width. Its most characteristic feature was the arrangement of six panels: two small ones at the top above four larger ones of about equal size. On early examples, from the eighteenth century, these panels were almost always of the raised and fielded type. In this, relatively thin chamfered edges fitted into slots in the surrounding frame timbers, while the thickness increased towards the centre until it was equal to the frame timbers. The joints between the frame's horizontal rails and vertical stiles, or muntins, and the thin edges of the panels were concealed by mouldings.

A curved canopy of delicate design for an early eighteenth-century house in Ashbourne, Derbyshire.

Most of the front doors of small- and medium-sized houses kept to this basic form with little change from around 1700 to about 1780. Until about 1730, the mouldings tended to have a simple quadrant or ovolo shape; after that the ogee became popular. The next major design change occurred in around 1790, when raised and fielded panels were superseded by flush panels. The basic layout remained popular, however, until the Regency period of the early 1800s when more flamboyant designs became fashionable, often incorporating circular panels or motifs in the lower half of the door.

After about 1837 until the First World War and beyond, the typical front door was characterised by four recessed panels: two large ones above, two smaller ones below. The timber was now machine cut, as were the mouldings, which were glued or pinned in position. Frosted or stained glass often took the place of the wood of the two upper panels. The development of strengthened glass during the first decades of this century made larger glazed door panels a practical possibility.

DOOR SURROUNDS AND PORCHES

Although plain square frames echoed the plainness of early doors in the smallest houses, door surrounds in better-class buildings were often moulded, and sometimes showed a Gothic influence which made them comparatively decorative. For example, door surrounds of the fourteenth and fifteenth centuries might be in the form of a tall, pointed arch, and by the late fifteenth century a shallower arch had appeared.

This design continued in use into the seventeenth century, with its outline becoming increasingly flatter. Ogee arches and shouldered arches (where the lintel is supported on curved brackets or corbels) were also used, the latter being typical of the late fifteenth and sixteenth centuries. As the Renaissance influence took over at the end of the seventeenth century, plain, square door frames became the most widespread. In the late eighteenth century, fashion dictated a complete classical frame to the doorway with pediment (low-pitched gable), straight-sided or segmental moulded pilasters (shallow columns attached to the face of a wall).

Porches were rare in the earlier periods, but a doorway might be protected from the weather by a lean-to roof supported on brackets. From these purely funtional beginnings, the porch evolved, and the opportunity was taken to introduce decorative elements reflecting the current architectural fashion. By the end of the seventeenth century, it might have a flat classical door hood, supported on console brackets, sometimes with elaborate ornamentation. By the end of the eighteenth century, open porches of ornamental cast iron were popular, their functional, draught-proofing origins apparently

A more robust, though still classical style canopy for a Queen Anne Revival house in Hampstead.

An Arts and Crafts-inspired door.

A 1930s door to a house in Hampstead; strengthened glass made such designs possible.

A fine ironwork porch to an early nineteenth-century house in Cheltenham.

forgotten. These trellis-type porches (as well as verandahs) were often added to older houses at this time.

As with regulations for windows, various building Acts discouraged the use of projecting timberwork on façades in London. After 1774, it tended to disappear completely, and door openings were given visual importance by the ornamental treatment of the surrounding masonry. As with other legislation, this change gradually affected building outside London.

DOOR FURNITURE

Early doors had wrought-iron strap *hinges* carried on iron brackets either attached on to heavy section wood jambs (vertical side members of a doorframe) or built directly into the stone walls. Following the Renaissance, the strap was superseded by variations on the 'H' and 'L' hinge, nailed rather than screwed to the doorframe; and in the eighteenth and nineteenth centuries, panelled doors were hung with iron and brass butt hinges. Early in the twentieth century, steel hinges began to be mass produced.

The earliest door furniture was made from wrought iron by the local blacksmith, who also produced the nails and bolts to affix it with. The Industrial Revolution of the late eighteenth century brought cast iron into use. With a Japanned or 'Berlin' black finish, this had the advantage of being both cheap and easy to clean. Brass, which was more expensive, remained popular among the wealthier Victorians. The Arts and Crafts Movement, and the Vernacular Revival which followed it, reinstated iron as a fashionable material.

Doors in ordinary houses of the Middle Ages were probably held shut by a wooden *latch* on the inside face of the door. This was succeeded by the simple wrought iron thumb or Suffolk latch, with security provided by a large, heavy wood or iron bar fixed across the door through slots in the walls either side. A more sophisticated form of security was the plate *lock*: used until the late fifteenth century, this had an iron bolt which engaged a striking plate fitted into the door jamb.

After the introduction of thick mahogany doors in the early eighteenth century, concealed mortise locks came into use. But surface locks, either encased in wood and painted to match the door, or with a brass coating, were also to be seen on front doors during the eighteenth and nineteenth centuries. Cast brass escutcheons or keyhole surrounds were also common. Steel locks became increasingly popular during the eighteenth to the nineteenth centuries, with mass-produced pressed steel latch surface locks coming into use from the 1880s.

Although there are earlier examples of *doorknockers*, they became widespread from the late seventeenth century as town populations grew. They were made from wrought iron or brass, with fairly simple variations on the ring handle with ornamentation on the backing plate. The S-shaped knocker appeared during Georgian times. Designs occasionally reflected historic events: a dolphin motif celebrated Nelson's victories, while a sphinx head alluded to the 1798 Battle of the Nile. On the whole, they followed the prevailing fashions, be they classical, Gothic or romantic.

Letterplates came into use after 1840 following the introduction of the penny post. The earliest examples are in plain cast brass, much smaller than today's models, and tend to have been fitted vertically on the centre line of the door. The establishment of the penny post also brought about the *numbering* of doors. Initially, numbers were engraved into the doors, but cast brass numbers were soon available, the earliest with spikes so that they could be hammered into the door.

From the 1820s, *bell pulls* became part of the range of door furniture. They were set into the masonry at the side of the doorframe, and the most common design was a circular knob set into a recessed brass dish. This type continued, although with rather smaller designs, into Edwardian times and was adapted to electricity after about 1900.

7

THE INTERIOR

STAIRCASES

The very earliest stairs were upright poles with projecting pegs for the hands and feet; later, simple ladders were used and could still be found in cottages in the nineteenth century. But some medieval houses had a spiral staircase situated in a turret, and this more architectural form of staircase became widespread during the sixteenth and seventeenth centuries with the spiral made in solid timber or stone, and either sited next to the chimney stack or, sometimes, in the thickness of the wall. Spiral, also known as newel, stairs continued to be constructed in smaller houses right through to the eighteenth and nineteenth centuries, but framed stairs, with treads and risers sturdily made in oak, started to appear during the seventeenth century.

The structure of the framed stair allowed the development of the straight flight and the dog-leg (returning on itself with a landing half-way up the flight) from the 1600s. There are early examples of these forms in open stair wells, sometimes with the stairs rising round four sides, with quarter space landings in the corners. This type of stair, designed as a focal feature of the entrance hall, provoked an explosion of creative and exuberant carving. The fashion for the grand staircase in large houses did not mean the demise of the simple or even the circular stair for, where upper-floor corridors did not exist, a modest extra staircase could give access without having to pass through intercommunicating rooms.

The stair's string, the side-member stiffening the outside edge, was left closed (in its uncut away plank form) in smaller houses, but during the eighteenth century was superseded in larger houses by

Vernacular cottage staircases were steep, curving sharply up to the floor above.

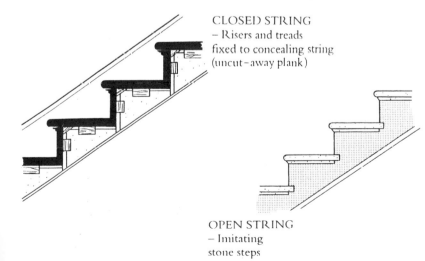

CLOSED STRING
– Risers and treads
fixed to concealing string
(uncut–away plank)

OPEN STRING
– Imitating
stone steps

Changes in staircase construction.

the cut-string stair. In this design, the string is cut away to follow the zigzag line of the steps, with the treads projecting slightly beyond it and capped with a nosing.

Balusters (posts supporting a handrail) and newel posts (posts at the top or bottom of a flight of stairs) offered an opportunity for decoration which craftsmen through the centuries have rarely been able to resist, and the patterns used naturally reflect the passing fashions. Early ornaments, or finials, for newel posts were in a simple circular acorn shape but, as wood-turning developed, more elaborate shapes were produced. Staircases in grander houses of the early seventeenth century had some elaborate carving of allegorical and heraldic animals. By the 1620s, there were examples where separate balusters had been superseded by a continuous balustrade of elaborately carved boarding, and this vogue continued until the end of the century.

Changes in balustrade design.

THE DEVELOPMENT OF THE BALUSTRADE

WOODEN

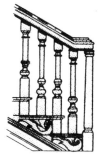

Elizabethan
(1550-1600)
The balusters are in the form of flat-section dwarf pilasters, and there is a square newel post surmounted by a simple vase-type finial

Jacobean
(1600-1650)
The string is carved, as is the newel post which is surmounted by an heraldic animal. The turned balusters were also used in earlier staircases

Late 17th century
(1650-1700) Even in early wooden stairs, a support of continual panelling, pierced by fretwork design, would be one of the accepted ways of supporting the handrail. By the late 17th century this type of screen had become an affair of elaborate carved foliage

WROUGHT IRON

Late 17th century
(1650-1700) The trend-setting King's staircase at Hampton Court with ironwork designed and made by the French master craftsman Jean Tijo[?]

Early Georgian *(1700-1750) From Abraham Swan's* The British Architect *(1738); note the reduced importance of the newel, the use of two balusters per step and carved ends or "brackets" to steps*

Late Georgian
(1750-1800)
The newel post has been replaced by a swirl of balusters

Early Georgian
(1700-1750)
A relatively simple design, incorporating an S motif

Late Georgian
(1750-1800) An elaborate affair, incorporating elements made of lead, designed by Robert Adam for Kenwood, Hampstead, built 1767-8

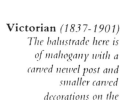

Victorian *(1837-1901)*
The balustrade here is of mahogany with a carved newel post and smaller carved decorations on the balusters

Regency *(1811-1837)*
The ultimate in simplicity with a mahogany handrail and straight iron balusters swirled at the bottom

The effect of the Renaissance was to reduce the newel post's importance and give the carved decoration of strings a lighter, more naturalistic style. Balusters became lighter too, perhaps with fluted, spiral or barley twist designs, and were two or three to a step. The handrail might finish with a scroll over the newel, which was sometimes reduced to a group of three or four balusters. Staircases became more curving, more elegant than their robust Tudor antecedents.

Simple balusters, alternating plain and barley twist patterns, at the top of a main staircase in a seventeenth-century house in Devizes.

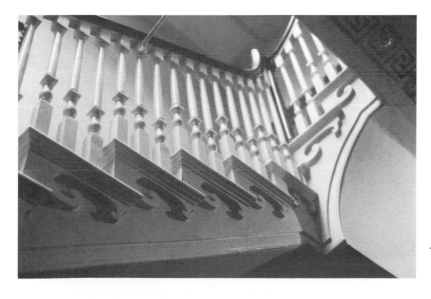

The eighteenth-century staircase, with three elegantly turned balusters for every tread, at No 1 Royal Crescent, Bath, headquarters of the Bath Preservation Trust.

Mahogany came into use for handrails after about 1720, but pine was utilised for other stair parts, except in the best-quality work which still required oak. From the late seventeenth century, iron also appeared in some staircases: an elaborate balustrade at Hampton Court was an early example. Ironwork designs became ever simpler, but after the slender, straight and square iron balusters of the Regency period, work in this material was limited and generally derivative. The increase of conservatories during the Victorian and Edwardian periods did, however, encourage a revival of the spiral staircase, this time made in cast iron.

A fine decorative staircase, with an emphatic acorn for the newel post, in an 1880s terraced house in Cheshire.

Victorian staircases sported innumerable designs for balusters and newel posts (although, for these, the acorn again became a popular motif), with patterns that are generally more complex than those for modern staircases. Few innovative styles have emerged since the end

The superb Arts and Crafts staircase at Standen, built by the architect Philip Webb in 1892.

of the nineteenth century, with the chunky staircases of the 1930s Tudorbethan houses being perhaps the most retrospective in character. Even the open staircases of the 1960s might be said to be a throwback to earliest constructions, although that period's ranch-style balustrades may be one of this century's few new developments in staircase design.

WALL PLASTER AND DECORATIONS

The stairs from the 1930s house of W F Crittall. Modern in style and utilising metal framework rather than conventional wooden banisters.

The current surface of plastered walls may well not be the original one, for coats of later plaster have often been applied over the top of earlier ones. Since earliest times, internal walls have almost invariably been plastered, although ashlar stone was sometimes simply limewashed. Where plaster was applied to studwork walls, rushes were an early form of lathing, but by the eighteenth century plaster was usually applied on rent or split laths, and sawn laths were used from the late nineteenth century.

Painted decoration on plain plastered walls, as well as beams or panelling, appeared in many medieval houses. The painting might feature subjects ranging from flowers and figures, to architectural details and religious texts, but the style of the clothes or ornament depicted may be the only guide to dating. Such decorations have often been covered over later by layers of limewash, plaster or paint, so many may still remain to be discovered.

Although the phrase 'decorative plasterwork' brings to mind Victorian and Edwardian designs for most people, the craft has a much longer history. A few examples survive from the fifteenth century, and it seems to have been quite widespread by the 1600s. During the seventeenth century, plaster was generally composed of lime, earth and hair, supported on laths, wattle or reeds. Although some ornament was cast, much of the work was modelled *in situ*, which gives it a particularly irregular, lively quality.

A fine decorative plaster ceiling at Holme Lacy in Hereford. It dates from the seventeenth century, long before mass-produced fibrous plasterwork made ceiling ornament commonplace right down the social scale.

The plasterwork in some medieval buildings imitates ashlar stone, timber-frame or textile hangings, but Tudor designs were more elaborate, with the houses of the wealthy having some fine, ornate schemes. The middle years of the seventeenth century saw more austere plasterwork but, after the Restoration, it once again became more complex, and the rebuilding after the Fire of London provided much interesting work by plasterers of considerable competence. As the influence of Italian designers made itself felt following the Renaissance, stucco (which contains no animal hair but relies on armatures of wood or metal) was also used. The more fragile-looking, high-relief plasterwork of this period is likely to be supported on such a skeleton, which may become visible if the plasterwork deteriorates.

During the eighteenth century, further variations in materials were introduced, including papier mâché, and new compositions such as Roman cement (hard hydraulic lime). Use of Portland cement in the 1800s produced harder plasters which were finished with a trowel to provide a smooth, regular surface, achieving a similar effect to the gypsum-based plasters used today.

Fibrous plasterwork is cast from a mould to be fixed in position later. Although there was some fibrous plasterwork in medieval times, it was limited to small bands and simple plaques. Until the middle of the nineteenth century, the materials used for moulds (wood, wax, plaster and iron) were somewhat inflexible, but since 1840 gelatine, and then rubber, have been used, and more innovative plasterwork has been produced.

During the late nineteenth and early twentieth century, lightweight casts, reinforced with hessian scrim, were mass-produced and large, inexpensive, elaborate designs became hugely popular. Plasterwork's heyday continued into the 1930s, when it was used to add individuality to houses and glamour to the new cinemas; but after the Second World War, the popularity of decorative plasterwork declined. Nowadays, Georgian- and Victorian-style fibrous plasterwork detail is readily available for the restoration/nostalgia market.

WOODWORK

Each house's decorative woodwork (internal doors, architrave, skirting boards and so on) will have originally reflected the prevailing fashion of its time. But, like the less-fixed elements of interior decoration, it may well have been changed to follow more recent tastes: for example, the complex mouldings of Victorian times were often replaced by the streamlined simplicity of the 1960s. On the other hand, most decorative woodwork is available today in traditional patterns, so something that looks as if it should be authentic, may be a very recent addition.

Panelling, easily moved from one venue to another, is not a foolproof guide to dating your house. But since original panelling

was generally used prior to the mechanisation of the timber industry, at least recently produced introductions can usually be spotted, either because they look too regular and are obviously machine-made, or because they have been over antiqued to give too rustic a finish.

From the fifteenth to the seventeenth century, non-loadbearing internal walls were either timber-framed with wattle and daub filling, or made from timber alone to make a *plank and muntin* wall. In the latter, timber uprights (or 'muntins') were attached to horizontal members at top and bottom and had grooved vertical edges so that thinner planks could be slotted in. Although the muntins were left plain in very simple work, they were often chamfered, and sometimes moulded. In modest cottages, this form of wood partition continued into the 1800s, with painted softwood superseding oak after the seventeenth century, and the muntins becoming lighter in section.

Romantic conjecture, rather than historical accuracy, is the hallmark of many interior restoration schemes through the centuries. Boscobel House, in Shropshire, was visited by Charles II in the seventeenth century and its nineteenth-century owners aimed to return it to how it was at that time although many of their ideas were based on fiction.

An original dark oak plank and muntin screen in a fifteenth-century Kent house.

Panelled room in an seventeenth-century house in Devizes.

More decorative timber walls, true *panelling*, had been introduced in the Middle Ages, but it was not until the Tudor period that it became at all usual in smaller houses. Oak or other native hardwoods were used; decoration was simple and limited to the framing members which surrounded the small panels. As the mouldings developed the framing members were mitred, and eventually the panels might be 'raised' so that their centre was level with the face of the framing members, while the edges were thin enough to fit into slots in the frame. *Linenfold* panelling, where the panels were carved to look like folded cloth, developed from this and became a popular style with the Tudors and Stuarts, who loved ornate carving and seem to have been fascinated by drapery.

As classical influences made themselves felt in the seventeenth century, linenfold fell from favour, although raised panelling remained popular. Panels became larger and were decorated with classical mouldings, with prestigious houses having panelling schemes that were worked out as architectural compositions. As with timber elsewhere in the house at this time, oak was less frequently used and painted softwoods, particularly pine, became more common.

From the eighteenth century, panelling in small houses often took the form of plain, vertical boarding (matchboarding), recalling the days of plank and muntin. But for the more affluent eighteenth-century homeowner, ornamental plasterwork and wallpapers pushed panelling out of popularity. As its fashionability waned, panelling's mouldings became generally finer and less assertive, although towards the end of the century it did display some Gothic detailing. In its diluted form, panelling might appear as a dado (from floor up to waist level), and this fashion continued into the nineteenth century, when splitting the wall surface into different sections became a vogue.

The Victorians also had a taste for dado rails, picture rails and skirting boards, as well as elaborate architraves surrounding doors and windows. The patterns were complex and the range available extensive, but many were removed or replaced when mid–twentieth taste could not tolerate such fussiness.

FIREPLACES

Like doors and windows, fireplaces have been vulnerable to changes in fashion. An inglenook may have been recently opened up to reveal the original beam damaged or missing, and the fireplace may now be very much a modern reconstruction. Georgian fireplace reproductions abound, some very convincing, and only evidence of changes to the surrounding skirting board may point to its real history. A Victorian fireplace is more likely to be authentic, but it may not necessarily be the same age as the rest of the house.

Early fires, set on the floor in the centre of the main room, have left little evidence other than blackened roof timbers. It was not until Norman times that fireplaces became part of the construction of a house and started to evolve as architectural features. Either built into the wall or given a projecting canopy, these structures might be of stone in better-class houses, but the majority were (like many contemporary chimneys) timber-framed. To help fire-resistance, they were covered with plaster on the outside and pargeting (mortar) on the inside.

Early fireplaces had stone or timber lintels, sometimes in the shape of a flattened-type Tudor arch. Fireplaces were large enough to take big logs and a substantial fire, which would usually be the only heating for the entire house: upstairs rooms would be warmed by radiated heat from the chimney stack. Such spaciousness allowed the development of the inglenook, almost a room within a room, where the occupants could gather close to the heat and out of the draughts. To reflect heat and protect the rear wall, there might have been a freestanding iron fireback, and perhaps a bread oven, or a compartment for the curing of ham, would have provided simple but valuable catering facilities in the wall to one side of the fire. These may have been incorporated into an older fireplace during the eighteenth or early nineteenth centuries, and a change in brickwork will show whether this is the case.

The inglenook continued in vernacular buildings well into the nineteenth century, but in houses of pretension it was soon to be replaced by more decorative fireplaces influenced by Renaissance design. However, the inglenook did see a minor revival in the houses of the fashionable during the nineteenth century, just as it was passing from common usage. Many inglenooks have been filled in to accommodate smaller fireplaces suitable for coal fires.

The influence of the Renaissance coincided with the introduction of coal as a domestic fuel, a material which could be burnt in grates within smaller fireplaces. The combined effect on fireplaces in polite houses during the eighteenth century was quite revolutionary: the desire for symmetry dictated the positioning of fireplaces, and interest in classical architecture was reflected as the mantelshelf took on the appearance of a pediment, supported by pilasters on either side of the fire. The fashionable choice of materials for fire surrounds was inspired by classicism too, with carved stone and marble the most popular at this time, but cheaper alternatives in Coade stone, plaster, gypsum and painted wood were also available. Structurally, these smaller openings were spanned by brick arches.

During the seventeenth century, there had been various experiments to control smoke and prevent heat loss, including baffle plates and an early type of the metal canopy that has persisted through to this century. But it was Count Rumford who, in 1799, published an essay, *Upon Fireplaces*, and earned himself the title 'apostle of fireplace comfort'.

He put forward a fireplace design in which the cross-sectional area of the flue (chimney shaft) was one-tenth of the area of the fireplace opening (earlier flues had been one-sixth), and introduced a constricted throat between the fireplace and its flue that transferred more heat back into the room rather than allowing it to rise freely up the chimney. To help prevent rain falling on to the fire, a smoke shelf was situated behind the throat. In addition, the Rumford fireplace itself was smaller, further forward into the room, and had an angled back and sides.

Existing fireplaces were often modified to incorporate these new ideas: masonry was added at the back of the fire to bring it further forward into the room and openings were reduced by installing hob grates (brick box with metal fronts) at either side. In later versions, hobs had doors and could be used as ovens.

By the beginning of the eighteenth century, the grate with cooking facilities had evolved into a range of sorts, with a cradle of iron bars resting on legs, before which meat could be roasted. Hooks suspended a spit, trivets supported pots and kettles. After the middle of the century, the range was improved with front panels of cast iron, and the first patent for a range with an oven was taken out in 1780. Ranges with built-in boilers followed within a few years and became a complete, though still relatively inefficient, item of kitchen equipment made to fit all sizes of fireplace opening and all pockets.

The open range, where the fire remained open to the chimney, was made throughout the nineteenth century and was the typical fitting for the working-class terraces. The closed range, which had a hot plate on the top with removable lids for faster boiling, was more expensive and confined to better-class houses. By the beginning of the twentieth century, gas and electricity were challenging the solid-fuel cooker, which might well have totally disappeared had it not been for the introduction of the Aga in 1929. This product has always been an expensive item and cheaper alternatives were soon developed in the form of the Rayburn and the Esse.

The inventive Victorians used cast iron to develop numerous variations to aid cooking on open coal fires, often combining ornament with utility. But their fireplaces also reflect the passing fashions of the time from the compact, delicate designs in the wake of the Regency, through the retrospective medieval look of the Gothic Revival to the heavier designs towards the end of the century. Throughout the period, fireplace openings were often supported on iron chimney bars.

From the 1860s, fireplaces displayed narrow panels of tiles on either side of the fire, and the Art Nouveau period at the turn of the century saw some very fine tile designs. After the 1880s, rectangular openings were in favour, and again Art Nouveau stimulated some innovative and unusual fireplace designs, with embossed copper hoods sometimes a decorative feature.

After the First World War, scaled-down inglenook fireplaces again appeared, this time in the Tudorbethan suburbs but, during this period, coal was challenged by gas and electricity. The most popular fireplace became the reinforced concrete slab covered completely with brown and cream speckled tiles, a fashion which reached its peak in about 1935. There was also a strongly nostalgic streak the Georgian-style fireplaces still being produced in marble and wood.

FLOOR MATERIALS

Earliest ground floors (and in some regions those at first-floor level too), were either beaten *earth* or lime ash. In medieval times, the peasant's hovel and the utility rooms of the middle-class manors would still have been earth, covered with rushes or straw, which could be replaced regularly with clean, sweet-smelling new material. Although some remain, most floors of this type have since been either covered over with tiling or stone flags, or have been removed in favour of wood or concrete.

Earth floors needed to include materials to help them hold together well so that they were not constantly crumbling and spreading dust. Clay, lime and animal blood were among the consolidants used, and these can be tested for by your local conservation officer, if you suspect that you may have an original earth floor. Accurate dating of an earth floor, however, is impossible.

Stone has been used for flooring in Britain since the time of the Romans, and is still available today. So, again, a stone floor will give little indication of a particular date although, after the beginning of the nineteenth century, solid floors generally were reserved only for the service areas of house. Used in all types of housing, stone flags were often laid direct on to earth and subject to damp conditions which have gradually destroyed them, so existing flags are quite likely to be replacements. The use of *bricks* for flooring, while not enjoying the same contemporary interest as stone, also spans a broad period and this material likewise suffers deterioration through damp.

As well as introducing stone flagged floors, the Romans also developed the British ceramics industry. However, it was not until the seventeenth century that floor *tiles* were used widely for the ground floors of secular buildings, while in the eighteenth century they were sometimes even used on the first floor, which was supported by the vaulting of the floor below. Before the beginning of the Industrial Revolution in the nineteenth century, tiles were generally plain squares, thick and often made in the locality, which gave them a colour and texture typical of the area's clay characteristics.

The cheaply priced tiles made possible by the Industrial Revolution brought them into popular use as a floor covering. For hall floors, plain square tiles of red, black and buff colour were often combined with other geometric shapes – triangles, rhomboids and chevrons – and laid surrounded with a row or two of small decorative border tiles. But for many pattern-loving Victorians, plain tiles could not compete with the 'encaustic' designs which began to be produced from the 1830s, and remained a favourite covering for hall floors over the next 50 years or so.

In the encaustic production process, recessed areas were pressed into tiles and the hollows filled with 'slip' (liquid clay) of a contrasting colour. The technique allowed simple bold patterns, such as fleur-de-lis and stylised flowers, which proved hugely popular. As the century progressed, encaustic tiles were pressed from dust clay, which made them even cheaper. The manufacturer Maw & Co used this more economical technique to make tiles that simulated mosaic work. In this, tiles were impressed with mosaic patterns which were filled with different colours of dust clay; then, after the tiles were laid, lines indented between the different pseudo 'tesserae' were filled with cement. The result was most convincing, and many a Victorian 'mosaic' hall floor is, in fact, simple encaustic tiles using this cunning design.

Plainer tastes since the 1930s have limited the use of ceramic floor tiles largely to the traditional 'quarry' type, still in production today. With such a timeless design, it is difficult to date quarry tiles. However, if they were laid more than 50 years or so ago, they are likely to be in a lime mortar, which will come away far more easily and cleanly than more recent mortar mixes, which contain cement.

Like timber-frame buildings, early *timber* floors reveal a complex choronolgy of different joints which would require a book in themselves; early floors also have wooden pegs (rather than nails) and may bear carpenter's marks. Until the sixteenth century, joists were laid broad side down rather than on their edge, and were large and often irregular timbers.

Oak has long been the preferred timber for British building work, but by the 1600s it was becoming more scarce. Other woods (such as elm) and foreign timber, which had been imported into Britain since the thirteenth century, were used increasingly. Imports of Scandinavian and Baltic pine became significant in the early eighteenth century, and its use increased until, by the end of the century, it had generally replaced oak as the usual timber for floors. Eighteenth century planks are generally wider than those used today.

After the Fire of London, the 1667 Rebuilding Act prohibited the use of beams spanning on to the heads of doors and windows, instead they spanned on to brick piers, providing a self-supporting structure for the floors. Aside from this legislation, the detail of floor construction remained relatively individual and varied until the mechanisation of the timber industry took place in the nineteenth century. The floor was often more flexible, or bouncy, too, as it was not geared to take the amount of furniture that the average home holds today. However, in the middle-class houses of the eighteenth century, the first floor (or 'piano nobile') became the place for the major rooms where most of the household's public life took place. As such, they required stronger floors, supported by large beams.

But the only major design change to timber floors occured in the first half of the nineteenth century, when the single-joisted floor started to replace the framed floor as the usual form of construction. The single-joisted floor, stronger and economical with wood, was designed to carry specific loads without having to be reinforced. Its joists span from front to back, bearing on external walls and the central spine wall. In the framed floor, load-bearing beams span from the front to the back of the building, or from side to side, and the joists bear on to them. Framed floors fall into two categories: in the single-framed floor, single joists span between the beams; in the double-framed floor, separate floor and ceiling joists span across in either the same direction or at right angles.

Under the first floor is the ground-floor ceiling, often now subject to today's fashion for exposed *beams.* But not all old beams were meant to be seen, and unless your house was really built before the Georgian period, exposed beams may be a false indication of age. When the underside of a supporting beam was designed to be exposed, it is carefully finished: it might be chamfered or moulded, carved or even painted with decorative motifs.

Although the beams of many small houses may often be rough and plain, some have shaped corners and the style of shaping can be used as a guide to dating. Deep chamfers, with a good deal of beam cut away, indicate the sixteenth century but, later, chamfers became progressively smaller. Chamfering does not usually run right to the end of a beam, but stops just before it meets the wall. The style of these 'stops' was quite plain in early examples, but became more elaborate later in better-class houses, where the beams may also be moulded. Gothic mouldings prevailed until the early sixteenth century; after that they show a classical influence.

As ornamental plaster ceilings became fashionable during the late seventeenth century, exposed timber ceilings became less common and, by the eighteenth century, they were rare in all but the smaller houses. Beams were cased in plaster or boarding, or hidden above ceilings wherever possible, and the obtrusive beams of many older houses were concealed as they were considered to be unsightly and unfashionable during the eighteenth and nineteenth centuries.

LOOR LEVELS

A change in floor levels may indicate that parts of the house are different ages, or that they have changed their use. In a long house, for example, the byre was often at a lower level, so that there was no risk of the animal slurry draining into the human occupants' living quarters. Such animal quarters are sometimes converted into kitchens, but keep the step down.

8

WHAT DOCUMENTS CAN TELL YOU

DEEDS AND OTHER DOCUMENTS

Deeds can be held by the householder, his/her solicitor, his/her
mortgage company or bank, and sometimes copies of early deeds are
held by the Public Record Office, the borough authority, or the
estate of the descendants of the local lord of the manor. Deeds may
be very sparse documents, simply marking the more recent
transference of property from one owner to another, or a bundle of
miscellaneous bits and pieces which will take much sorting out and
yield lots of information. Where a house was once part of a larger
estate, the original deeds may remain with the original landowner.

In must also be remembered that many more properties were
tenanted rather than owned in previous centuries, and records of
such tenures will have been held by the local landlord. The nature of
ownership has changed, too. In medieval times, a house and land
were held in 'fee simple', with the occupier providing services of
some kind to the local lord. These services were attached to the
house rather than the individual, so the lord was keen to be aware of
any transfer of property and the handing over of possession was done
in a public ritual before witnesses.

By the twelfth century, there was likely to be written evidence of
such transactions in addition, and these took the form of deeds of
gift or 'charters of feoffment'. Written deeds were not actually
required until the end of the seventeenth century but, even so, early
examples have not fared well: too often they have been destroyed by
damp or fire, or stored in attics where they have been eaten by mice.
The legal jargon of modern deeds can be bad enough, but early
documents may be in Latin or an English which is very alien to us

today. In addition, they will be handwritten quite possibly with forms of letters and numbers which may have changed beyond recognition through the centuries.

Deciphering old documents requires patience. Work from the letters or words that you recognise, but try not to leap to conclusions or take things for granted. Get the general sense of the material, copying out the sections that you understand and leaving gaps for those bits that puzzle you. This process will help 'get your eye in' to the style of the writing, so that when you return to the gaps the words should seem clearer and will hopefully fall into place within the flow of the whole.

LOCAL SOURCES

Many *local libraries* have excellent reference sections on local history and genealogy, and you should explore this convenient source very thoroughly first before planning trips elsewhere.

Even if the material at the local library does not actually provide information about your house in particular, it will make you aware of the possibilities, sources and contacts, while it is also likely to be a good starting point for old photographs and illustrations of the area.

Often the library will have informative local history booklets, available for a small sum and lovingly prepared by amateur historians, who may be part of a *local history group* . Such a group can be a great source of inspiration and a provider of fascinating detail. The members, and perhaps the authors of the any booklets, will probably be delighted to expand your knowledge of your particular property and its previous occupants.

The local library may also be the repository for collections of *family papers*, which may include certificates of birth, baptism and so on, as well as accounts, wills, diaries and, perhaps, a family Bible with notes about major events inscribed on the fly leaf. The papers of *local businesses* may also have been deposited at the local library, and your house may be mentioned in material from its builder, the solicitor or estate agent when it was sold, or as the home of a worker. Alternatively, it may once have been commercial premises or served as some sort of institution.

Among the most important books the local library can make available to the house history researcher is the *Victoria County History* (VCH). This series covers most of the country, giving an account of its manorial history over many centuries and giving the names of those who owned the land.

Records of the county authority may be looked after by the *County Archivist* or the Clerk to the Council. Just what such a collection includes varies from area to area, but you might find local criminal court records, manorial rolls, parish registers, deeds, leases and manuscript maps.

Bound, archive copies of *local newspapers* are also likely to be available in the reference section of your public library. Going through these can be rather a lengthy task as it is easy to get distracted by gruesome stories, apparently included with some relish during Victorian times. Even if you cannot find anything directly relevant to your search, the articles will give a real flavour of what life was like in the area in times past.

Newspapers can also provide details of the sale of properties and advertisements for building workers for specific development projects. But births, deaths, marriages and anniversaries were less likely to be reported than now, for there were few provincial papers prior to about 1830 and, before an effective transport system facilitated the delivery of national newspapers, they tended to repeat national news for local consumption, rather than focusing on local issues as they do now.

You can use your current local paper, too, to gather information, by advertising or writing to the Editor asking if anyone can tell you any details about your house and its previous occupants.

The national collection of newspapers is held at Colindale in North London. However, the collection is not complete as it suffered losses as a result of bombing during the Second World War, and publishers' own records may be more complete.

The *County Records Office* (CRO) is usually part of the council offices in the county town. It is usually staffed by helpful and specially trained people who will be happy to help you with your task; they may even have a booklet available to give you some tips on how to carry out your research. Look through the CRO's index using the names of landowners, discovered in the VCH, to see what relevant material is available: CROs have *Land Tax* rate collectors' books, and many also have special collections of material donated by local companies and estates. When you have pinpointed what might relate to your own property, you can then order the documents to be fetched from the store. Like most archive collections, your CRO will probably not allow biros or pens so, as well as a notebook, you should take pencils with you.

The Church has been a major landowner and *church records* can be extensive and carefully kept. Although they may have been deposited with the CRO or PRO, some are kept by the Church Commission's Record Office in London; if you write first explaining what you are looking for, they will advise if they can help and make an appointment for you. Church libraries are another possibility, but they may or may not be blessed with staff and resources.

Before the days of the County Court and the County Council, the negotiation of leases and the meting out of justice for less serious offences were dealt with by the local lord. These activities would have been noted in the *manor and court rolls* . Like deeds, the earliest rolls are in Latin on parchment, later ones in English on paper. They are generally neatly written and with fairly consistent spellings. After the Reformation, these rolls were considered less important and this form of record taking fell into disuse. The rolls and many other manorial records are held at repositories throughout the country, but a register of their whereabouts is held at the National Register of Archives.

*N*ATIONAL SOURCES

For access to the *British Library* (housed at the British Museum), you must apply in writing, specifying the purpose of your researches, and support your application with a recommendation from someone of recognised position who knows you personally. Details can be obtained from the Library, which also publishes a series of guides, some of which cover subjects such as sources for family history and family names.

Some of the reference books are available for readers to find themselves, but others must be ordered from stock rooms and located by the staff. A central catalogue lists the books available and a form must be filled in with the correct references. The book will be brought to you, but you may have to wait two or three hours – you can order books in advance (by post even) so that they will be waiting for you on your arrival. The size of this colossal library is what makes it seem slow, but is also its attraction, for (theoretically at least) it should have every book published since 1842, and a great many from before that time.

Among the other national libraries which you might find useful is the *Guildhall Library*, which has records of the City Livery Companies with apprenticeship and enrolment books, various London and provincial directories and poll books, and the list London City Inhabitants 1695. *Trade organisations, universities, private libraries* and *professional bodies*, such as the Royal Institute of British Architects, may all have material relating to your property or its occupants.

The *Domesday Book* was compiled in 1086 to detail feudal land and its potential for taxation. While it is extremely unlikely to mention your house, it gives a picture of estates at the time and a fascinating background to the country today. Fortunately for all of us who are not able to read easily through the original, Phillimore Books of Chichester publish a series of 34 texts with original descriptions of an area next to their translations into modern English, plus notes, maps, a glossary and an index of names and places.

The *Public Record Office* (PRO) works on much the same system as the CRO. You will need a reader's ticket, but this can be obtained at the reception counter. It is worth contacting the Search Rooms at Kew before you visit as they will send you an information leaflet and a map to help make your debut there less confusing.

Once there, Kew's helpful staff will order your required documents which will be delivered to a seat number in the reference room. A pocket bleeper will tell you when the material is ready for you and meanwhile you can explore, or eat in the restaurant. Among the useful materials at Kew are apprenticeship books and professional records, while tithe maps and tithe apportionments, which give names of owners and occupiers, can be examined in the Map Room.

Almost half a million structures are *Listed* by the DoE as being of historic importance. The initial survey was carried out between 1947 and 1969 and included some 120,000 buildings. A new survey, with broader criteria and calling for greater detail, was immediately begun and recently completed. The List covers all types of buildings from the grand to the extremely humble, but generally only exceptional buildings are included from Victorian times and onwards.

Apart from giving the country a record of what historic buildings it still retains, the List gives home owners the opinions of the DoE's inspectors as to a house's age and interest. The word 'opinions' should be emphasised here, for often dates have been decided after a fairly superficial external inspection. Thus an early building behind a later façade may well go undetected, and modern traditional style has been known to fool the unwary, too. The Lists are available for inspection at County and District Council Offices.

The Royal Commission on Historic Monuments also records and analyses period houses, but on a less systematic basis. They can make available a range of material which includes reports and inventories, photographs and some plans, and have detailed studies of specific areas or types of building.

Since 1841, a *Census* has been taken every 10 years; while the material is initially confidential, after 100 years it is released and the census returns up to 1891 can be examined in your local library, CRO or PRO. To make use of the information presented in the census, you need to know the name of your parish and then check through that listing for the address or, if you know it, the name of the owner at that time. The census lists the number of people living in a property, and while the inclusion of your house on a list for the first time can indicate the date of its construction, the information will also give some insight into who lived there and possible relationships with their neighbours.

*V*ISUAL SOURCES

Before you start looking at old *Ordnance Survey* (OS) maps, get well acquainted with the placing of your house on the modern version, and its relation to topographical features, roads, railways and canals. The location of other buildings, and even field patterns, will have changed over the decades and should not be used as a foolproof way of deciding which of the properties marked is your own.

The Ordnance Survey was actually founded in 1791, putting map making on an official footing, although privately produced county maps continued into the nineteenth century. By 1840 most of England and Wales had been mapped at a 1-inch scale in what is now called the 'Old Series', or 'First Edition'. From mid-Victorian times through to World War One, a series of 25-inch-to-1-mile OS maps was produced which shows properties in great detail. Some of these can be bought as reprints from booksellers, but if the map you want is not available, you should be able to look at it in your local County Records Office.

This is also where you should be able to find the relevant *tithe maps* . These are generally large and accurate, with each property clearly marked. Tithe maps were prepared in about 1840, when the traditional parish tithes were changed into a fixed annual charge for each property, but there is sometimes an earlier similar style map produced at about the time of the enclosures. Accompanying the tithe map will be a book of Apportionments giving the names of landowners and tenants, as well as the acreage and value of the property.

For about 300 years, farming was run by tenants of great estates and landlords needed regularly updated maps in order to keep their valuations current. If your property was once part of such an estate. it will appear on the *estate maps* which are often both detailed and decorative.

Photography developed from the middle of the nineteenth century onwards, and provides the most 'realistic' of all the possible records of the past. It is well worth tracking down previous owners, the authors of local history books, or the local history society, who may have photographic views which include your house, so that you can have copies made of any prints.

From the 1860s, picture postcards were produced, and one of the nineteenth century entrepreneurial companies in this area, Frith, have an archive on microfiche. Professional photographs of a different kind, those shot from the air, can show evidence of past buildings and field patterns that are invisible to us at ground level and place a house in its archaeological setting in a visually dramatic way. Aerial photography companies, such as Hunting Aerofilms of Boreham Wood, Hertfordshire, have archive material, while the National Monuments Record and Cambridge University Committee for Aerial Photography also have collections.

9

GENEALOGY: WHO LIVED HERE?

For many people the history of their house is really brought to life by knowing something of its past occupants. Genealogy, or the study of your ancestors, has become a popular pastime, and there are many guides for beginners, as well as local Family History Societies, about which your local library or record office will be able to give you full details. While you may have to slant the information to help you find out about the earlier occupants of your house rather than tracing back your own family tree, many of the sources and techniques remain the same.

Information from neighbours is a good starting point, so try talking to older neighbours who have been in the district some years. They may have first-hand knowledge of one of more of the previous owners of the house, not just names but interesting snippets that will give you a sense of the characters involved and, perhaps, details of work done on the house too.

If you feel talking to a neighbour could be a fruitful line of enquiry, it is worthwhile using a tape recorder so that you do not forget what has been said, or hinder the flow of reminiscences by asking them to wait while you write things down. However, even if you are using a tape recorder, it is well worth making some notes too, in case the machine lets you down in some way. Do not expect the information to be switched on immediately, to follow a coherent pattern or necessarily to be entirely correct, but it can be an entertaining start to your research and an insight into past lifestyles.

You may be able to speak to recent owners about their knowledge of the house when they lived there, and perhaps they will know also about its owners and condition before that. If you are not able to contact recent owners, they may have been local people who still have relatives in the area. Rejoice if past owners had an unusual surname, it will be so much easier to trace through local directories. If your house is in a small community, local shops, the post office and the public house will probably be able to provide a few details or names of folk who may help your researches – but pick a moment when these businesses are not too harassed to answer a few enquiries.

The outline of information gathered in this way can be checked at the *General Register Office* (in London and Edinburgh) where entries for births, marriages and deaths are held. There are separate indexes for these categories, filed chronologically and divided in quarter years. The index will give you a reference for a certificate; note down the details, fill in an application form and pay at the counter for a copy of the certificate. You can either have the certificate posted or pick it up in a few days. From the first certificate, you will be able to work slowly back through the family's records, which will supply not just names and dates, but also occupations and numbers of children. If your house remained in the ownership of one family for many years, your task becomes very much one of straight genealogy.

Local Register Offices are far less geared up for the public doing their own research, but if you know precise dates and are pretty sure of the possible parish where, say, a marriage took place, they may help you. However, you should ring and make an appointment first.

St Catherine's House in Kingsway, the London General Register Office, holds material from 1837, while at the Scottish Office registration started from 1855. Scottish certificates are very full and give lots of interesting detail, but the country's limited number of surnames can make research difficult. Registration in Ireland started in 1864, but certificates are not held in one filing system. Up until 1922, all entries are held under county in Belfast; those for southern Ireland after that date are kept in Dublin. Microfilm copies of some of the indexes at the General Register Office are available in some other parts of Britain; your local library should be able to tell you where and what would be your nearest source.

The Church of Latter Day Saints (Mormons) has some UK centres that also hold copies of some indexes, while others can obtain material for you (though it may take some time). As part of their faith, members of the church have to trace their own ancestors and these centres were initially created for use in their researches. Check in your local telephone directory and phone for an appointment.

Another source which you might find useful is the library of the *Society of Genealogists*, near the Barbican in East London. You can become a member, but the library is also open to non-members for a fee. A great many printed books on genealogy are housed here, but there is also a wealth of unpublished manuscript works, all available for reference direct from the shelves rather than having to order books and wait for them to be delivered to you by staff.

Among the material held there are parish records, poll books, the records of various national societies, and periodicals relating to professions, such as dentistry, law, the army, airforce and navy. There are also reference books on the peerage, heraldry, universities and the Inns of Court. The Society can also undertake research for you (for a fee), and provide names of researchers; it also publishes a guide to the Library and a list of the titles in its collection.

Records of wills proved in England and Wales since 1858 are held at *Somerset House* in London, and the entries can provide considerable information. The indexes are filed alphabetically under the name of the testator and according to the date when the will was proved. *District Probate Registries* also exist throughout England and Wales, but much of their material has been handed over to County Record Offices and it is worth checking out your local situation.

The information available from *Electoral Registers* can be fairly limited, as only those owning or tenanting large properties could vote in the early days and, although the system was gradually extended, it was not until 1919 that women over 30 got the vote and nine years later that the female age limit was dropped to 21. *Poll books* list qualified voters, and how they voted, before 1872. *Kelly's Post Office Directories* can be used in conjunction with local street directories to find an individual's occupation and address, although they do not list every inhabitant of a town or village.

Parish Registers are usually at the County or City Record Office (CRO), as well as at the local church. They may be more easily accessible at the CRO where there will be set opening hours and staff who are used to dealing with enquiries. Residence in a parish does not necessarily mean that the previous occupants attended the local church, however: they may have been non-church goers, or belonged to a different faith with a centre of worship further away. In addition, information tends to be less extensive and less precise: baptism and burial registers, for example do not give the dates of birth and death. Certificates and census returns will be more useful to you back to the dates when they started. For the period before that, when a high percentage of the population would regularly attend the local church, parish registers can be an invaluable source.

Parish registers date back to the middle of the sixteenth century, but many early records were transcribed during the reign of Elizabeth I. Very early entries will be in Latin, and records at many times were often ill-written and irregularly kept. Another difficulty is the variety of spellings for any one name, for an illiterate population knew their own names only through oral tradition, and the clerk would just have to guess at how they should be written. Many parish registers have now been published in printed form, so the researcher is spared the problems of deciphering alien handwriting.

ADDRESSES

Ancient Monuments Society, St Ann's Vestry Hall, 2 Church Entry, London EC4V 5HB. 071-236 3934.

British Library, British Museum, Great Russell Street, London WC1B 3DG. 071-636 1544.

British Newspaper Library, Colindale Avenue, London NW9 5HE. 071-636 1544

Cadw (Welsh Historic Monuments), Brunel House, 2 Fitzalan Road, Cardiff CF2 1UY. 0222 465511.

Church Commission's Record Office, 15 Galleywall Road, South Bermondsey, London SE16 3PB. 071-222 7010.

Church of Jesus Christ and Latter Day Saints Family History Centre, 64-68 Exhibition Road, Kensington, London W7. 071-589 8561.

Civic Trust, 17 Carlton House Terrace, London SW1. 071-930 0914.

Council for British Archaeology, 112 Kennington Road, London SE11. 071-582 0494.

Council for the Protection of Rural England, Warwick House, 25 Buckingham Palace Road, London SW1. 071-976 6433.

English Heritage, 23 Savile Row, London W1. 071-973 3000.

Francis Frith, The Old Rectory, Bimport, Shaftesbury, Dorset SP7 8AT. 0747 55669

General Register Office (Office of Population, Censuses and Social Surveys), St Catherine's House, 10 Kingsway, London WC2B 6JP. 051-471 4200.

Georgian Group, 37 Spital Square, London E1 6DY. 071-377 1722.

Guildhall Library, Aldermanbury, London EC2P 2EJ. 071-606 3030.

Historic Buildings and Monuments Scotland, 20 Brandon Street, Edinburgh EH3 5RA. 031–556 8400.

Hunting Aerofilms, Gate Studios, Station Road, Borehamwood, Hertfordshire WD6 1EJ. 081–207 0666.

Irish Georgian Society, Leixlip Castle, Leixlip, Co. Kildare, Ireland. 010 3531 6244211.

National Monuments Record, 23 Savile Row, London W1. 071–973 3500. National Library of Aerial Photography is located at: RCHME, Alexander House, 19 Fleming Way, Swindon SN1 2NG. 0793 414100.

National Register of Archives, Quality House, Quality Court, Chancery Lane, London WC2A 1HA. 071–242 1198.

Public Record Office, Census Room, Portugal Street, London WC2A. 081–876 3444.

Public Record Office, Ruskin Avenue, Kew, Richmond, London TW9 5DU. 081–876 3444.

Railway and Canal Historical Society, 17 Clumber Crescent North, The Park, Nottingham NC7 1EY. 0602 414844.

Royal Commission on Historical Monuments, 23 Savile Row, London W1. 071–973 3500. National Archaeological Record: 071–494 3998. National Buildings Record: 071–973 3148.

The Royal Institute of British Architects, 66 Portland Place, London W1N 4AD. 071–580 5533. (Also regional offices throughout the country).

Scottish Civic Trust, 24 George Square, Glasgow G2 1EF. 041–221 1466.

Society for the Protection of Ancient Buildings, 37 Spital Square, London E1 6DY. 071–377 1644.

Society of Genealogists Library, 14 Charterhouse Buildings, Goswell Road, London EC1M 7BA. 071–251 8799.

Twentieth Century Society, Environmental Institute, Bolton Road, Swinton, Manchester M27 2UX. 061–793 9898.

Vernacular Architecture Group, Brick Field, 20 Kiln Lane, Betchworth, Surrey RH3 7LX.

Victorian Society, 1 Priory Gardens, Bedford Park, London W4 1TT. 081–994 1019.

*B*IBLIOGRAPHY

*A*RCHITECTURAL BOOKS

Barley, M W, *The English Farmhouse and Cottage*, Routledge & Keegan Paul, London, 1976.

Brunskill, R.W, *Illustrated Handbook of Vernacular Architecture*, Faber, London, 1977.

Cook, Olive, *The English House Through Seven Centuries,* Penguin, 1984.

Cunnington, Pamela, *How Old is Your House?*, Alpha Books, 1980.

Insall, D W, *The Care of Old Buildings*, Architectural Press, London, 1958.

Iredale, David and Barrett, John, *Discovering Your Old House*, Shire Publications, 1991.

Mercer, Eric, *English Vernacular Houses*, HMSO, 1975.

Pevsner, N, *The Buildings of England Series*, Hamondsworth, 1951 seqq.

Powell, C, *Discovering Cottage Architecture*, Shire Publications, 1984.

Saunders, Matthew, *The Historic Home Owner's Companion*, Batsford, 1987.

Summerson, John, *Georgian London (revised edition)*, Barrie & Jenkins, London 1988.

Volumes of the Survey of the Royal Commission on Historical Monuments.

DOCUMENTARY RESEARCH AND GENEALOGY

Cox, J and Padfield, T, *Tracing Your Ancestors in the Public Record Office*, HMSO, 1981.

Gibson, J, and Peskett, P, *Record Offices and Where to Find Them*, Gulliver Publishing Co and Federation of Family History Societies, 1981.

Humphrey-Smith, C R, *A Genealogists Bibliography*, 1984.

Humphrey-Smith, C R, *The Phillimore Atlas and Index of Parish Register*, 1984.

Pelling, George, *Beginning Your Family History*, Countryside Books/The Federation of Family History Societies, 1980.

Spufford, P, and Camp, A J, *The Genealogists Handbook*, Society of Genealogists, 1969.

Thoyts, E E, *How to Read Old Documents*, Phillimore, 1980.

Willis, Arthur, and Tatchell, Molly, *Genealogy for Beginners,* Phillimore, 1984.

The Greater London Council Survey of London.

Royal Commission on Historical Manuscripts, *Record Repositories in Great Britain*, HMSO, 1979.